A Big Mandala Coloring Book

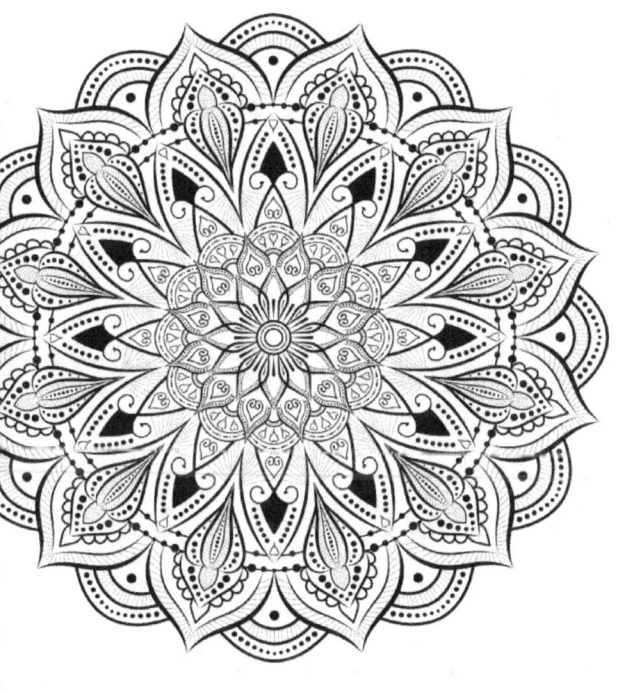

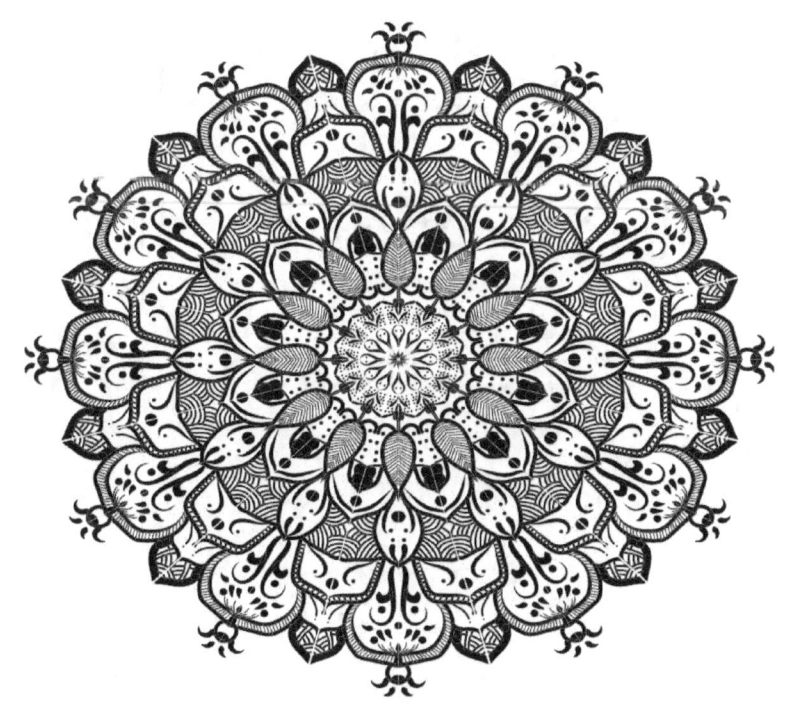

100

BEAUTIFUL MANDALAS

Big Mandala Coloring Book for Adulte With 100 Highly detailed, Unique and extremely Beautiful Floral Mandalas for Inspiration, Exitement, Joy aMediation, concentrate and Relaxation.

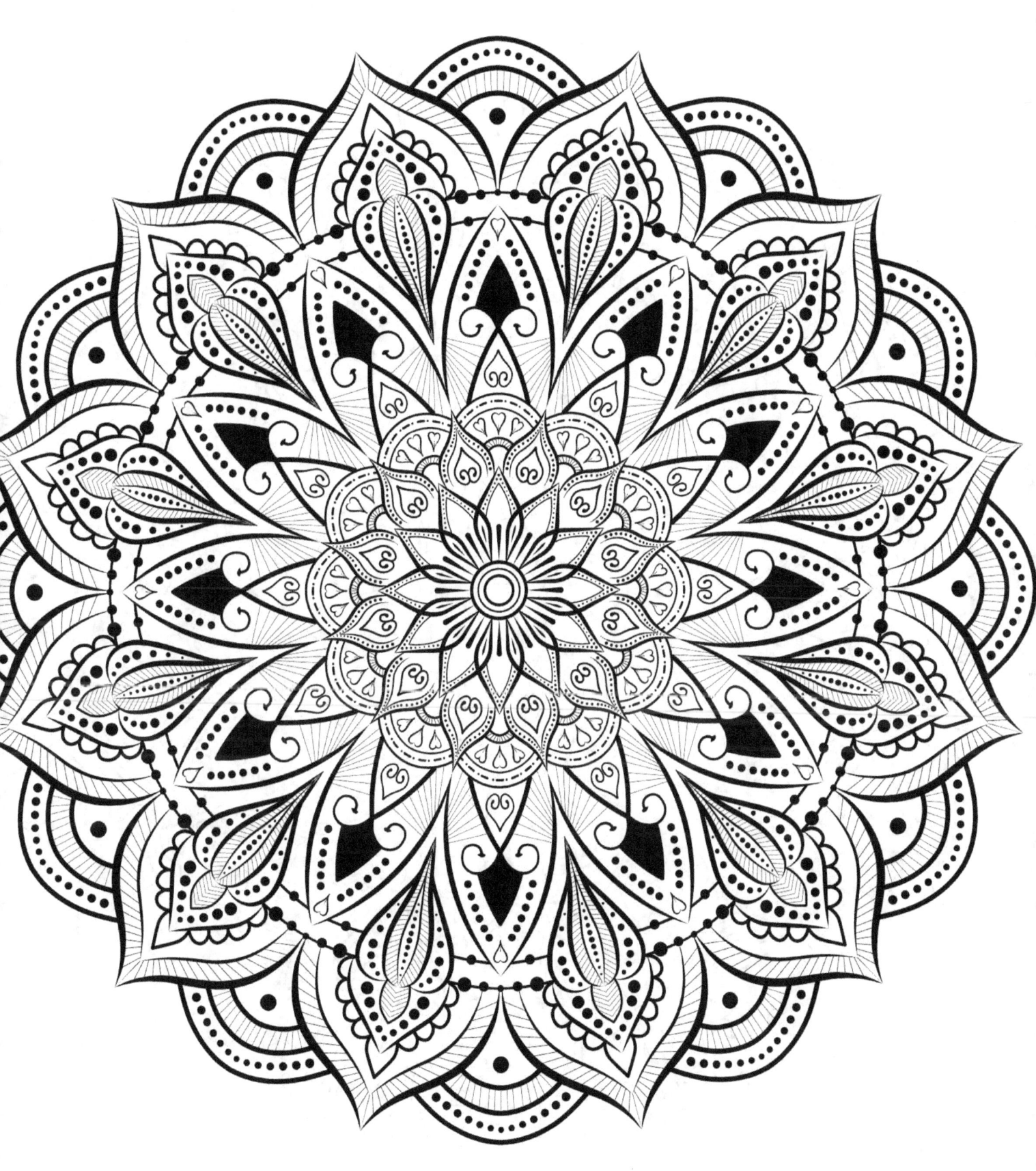

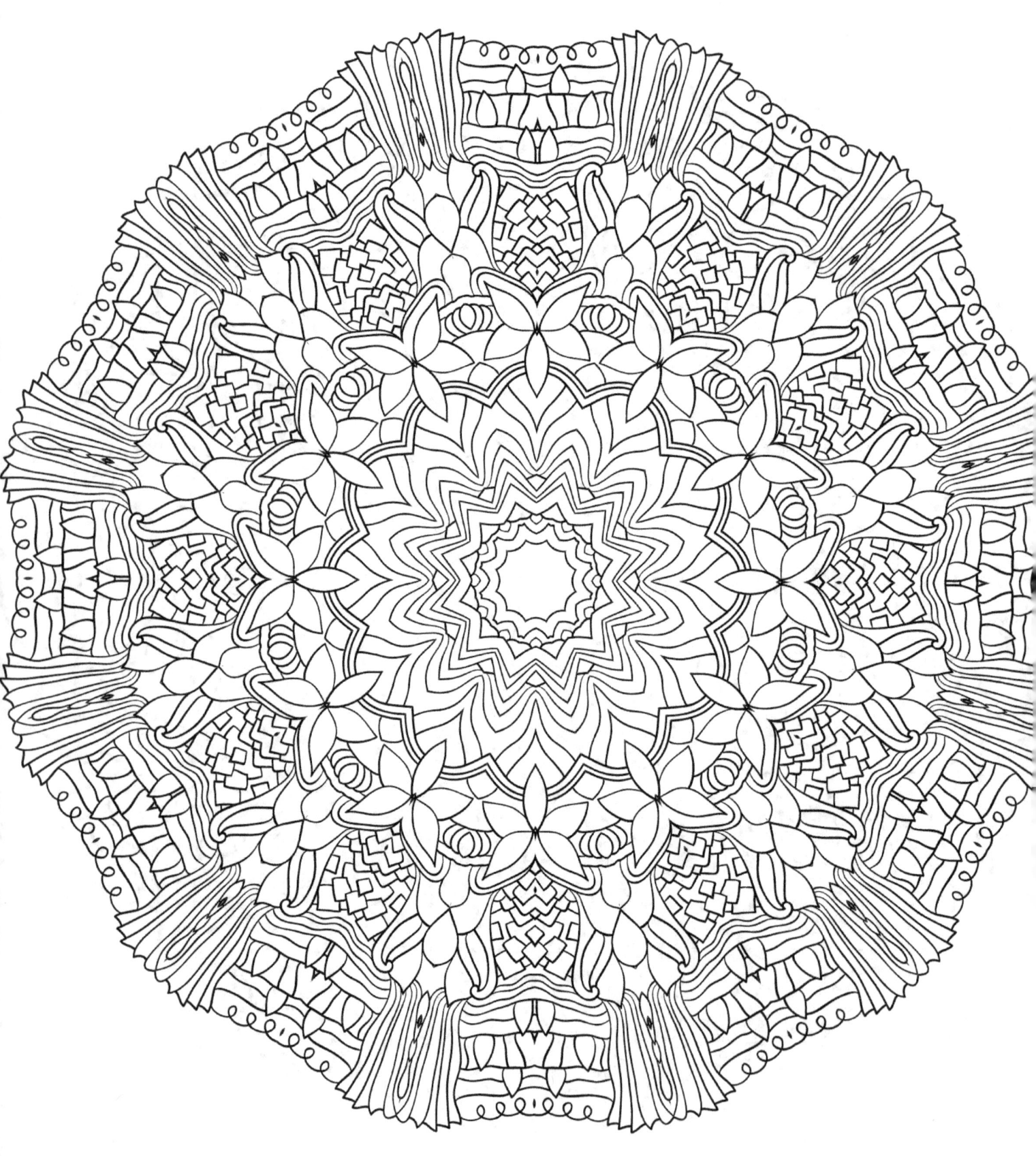

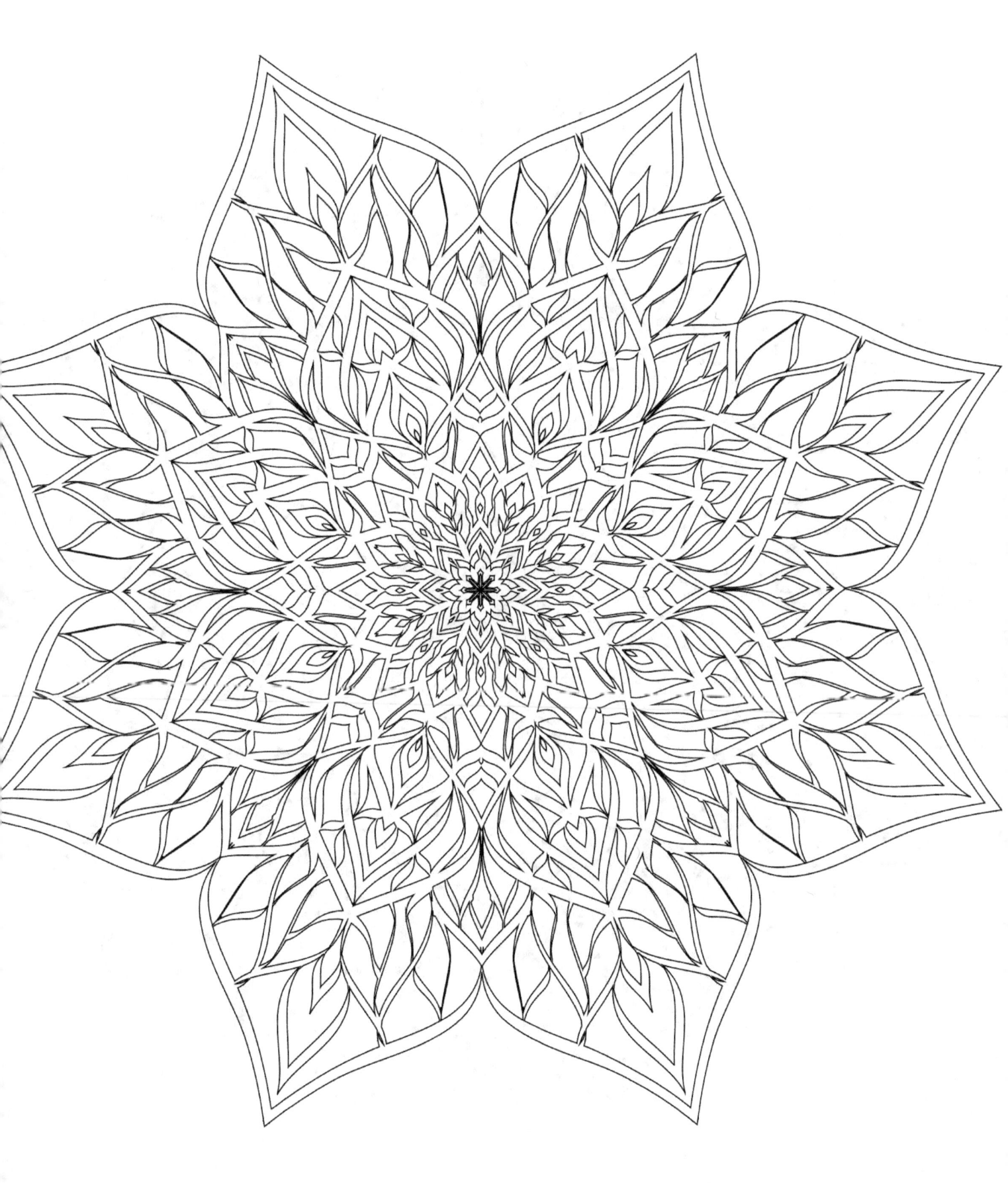

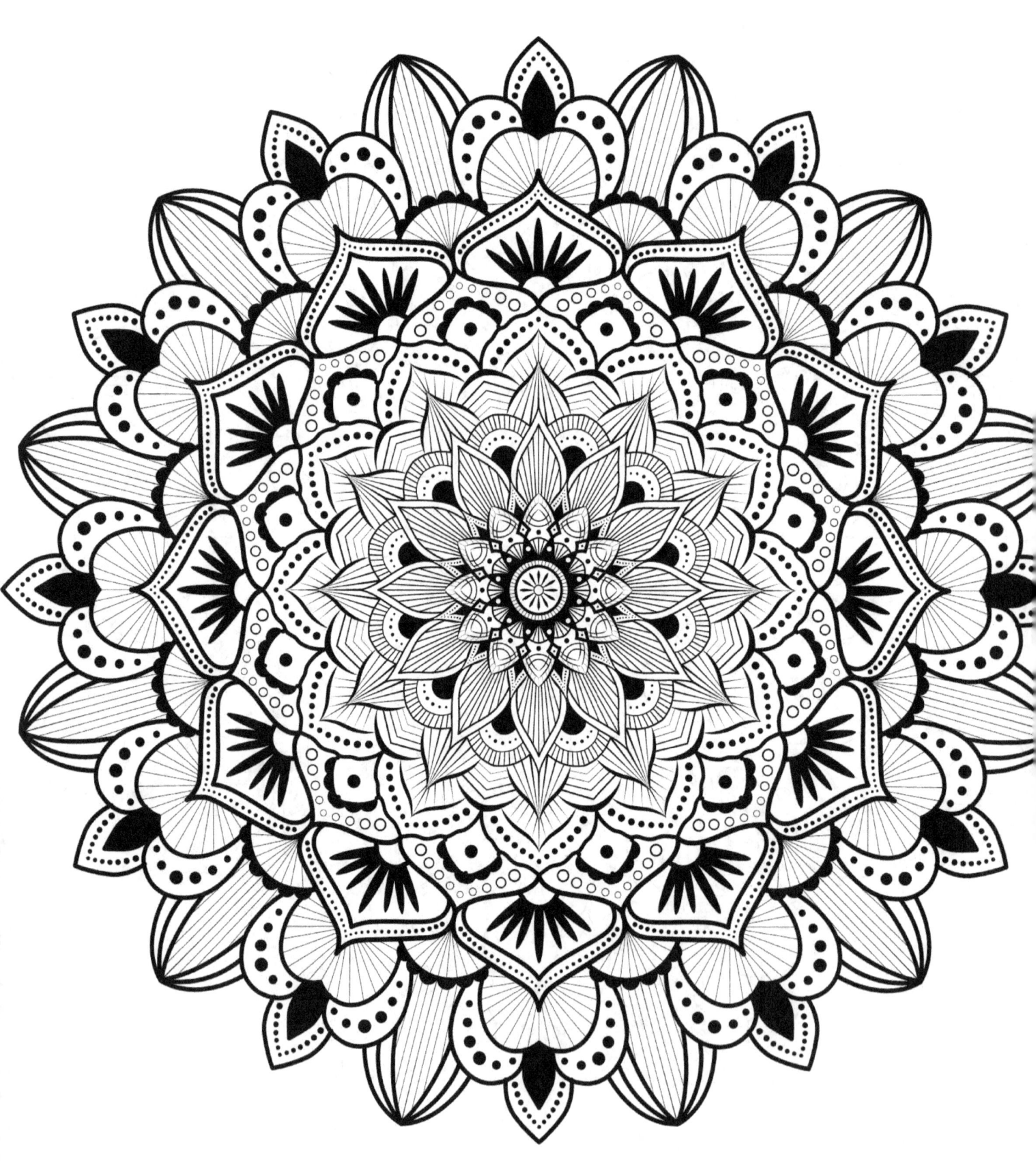

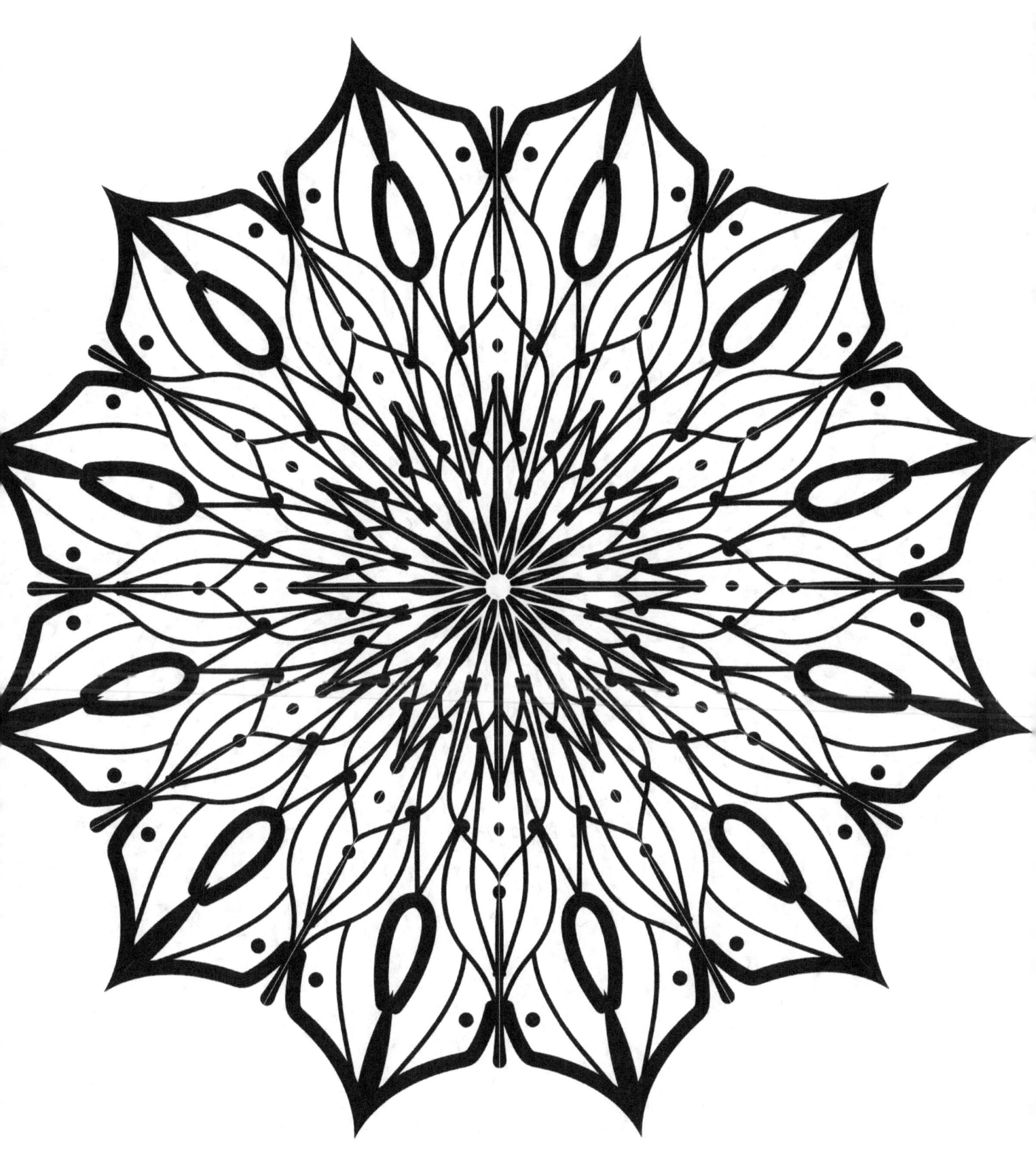

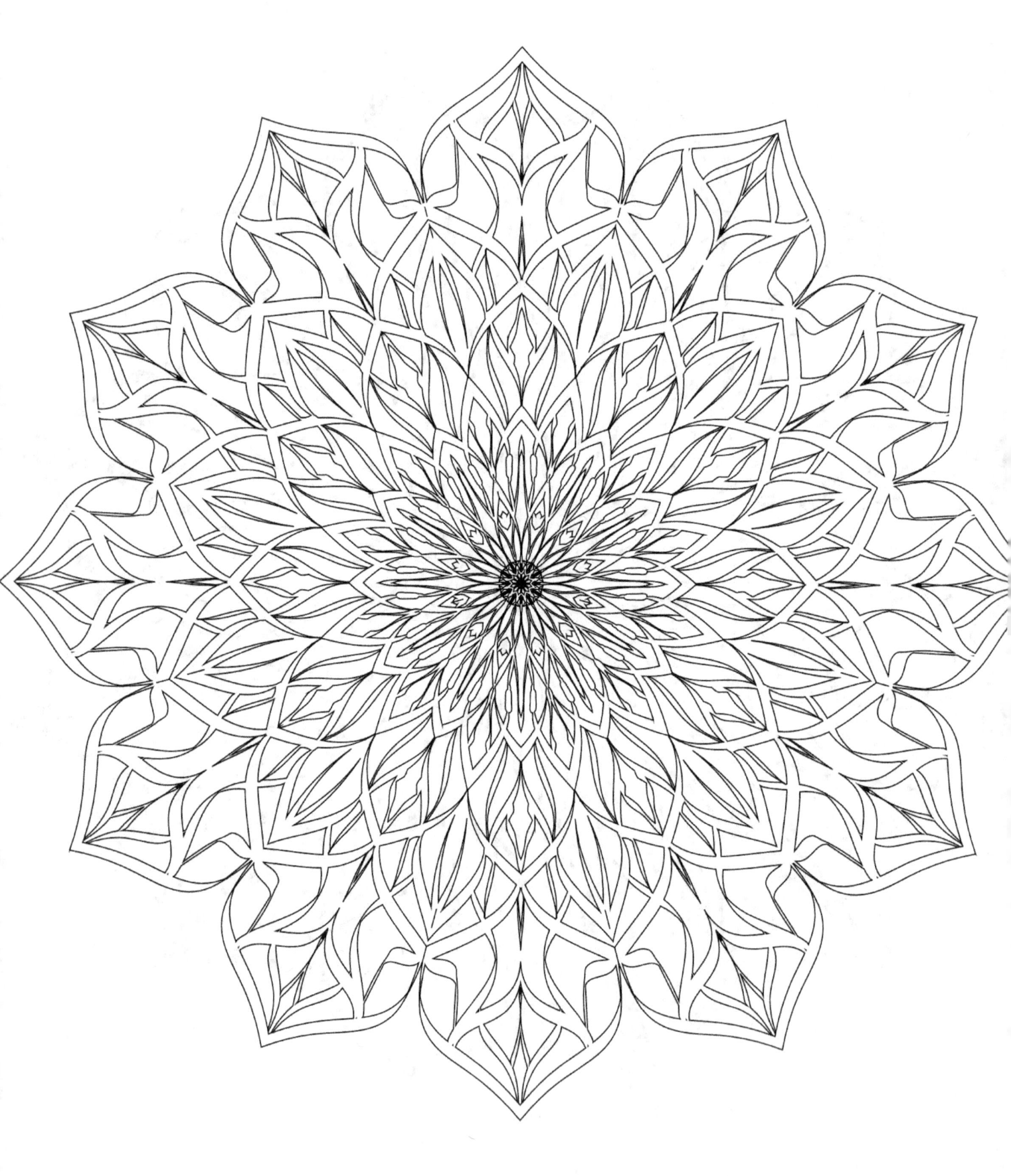

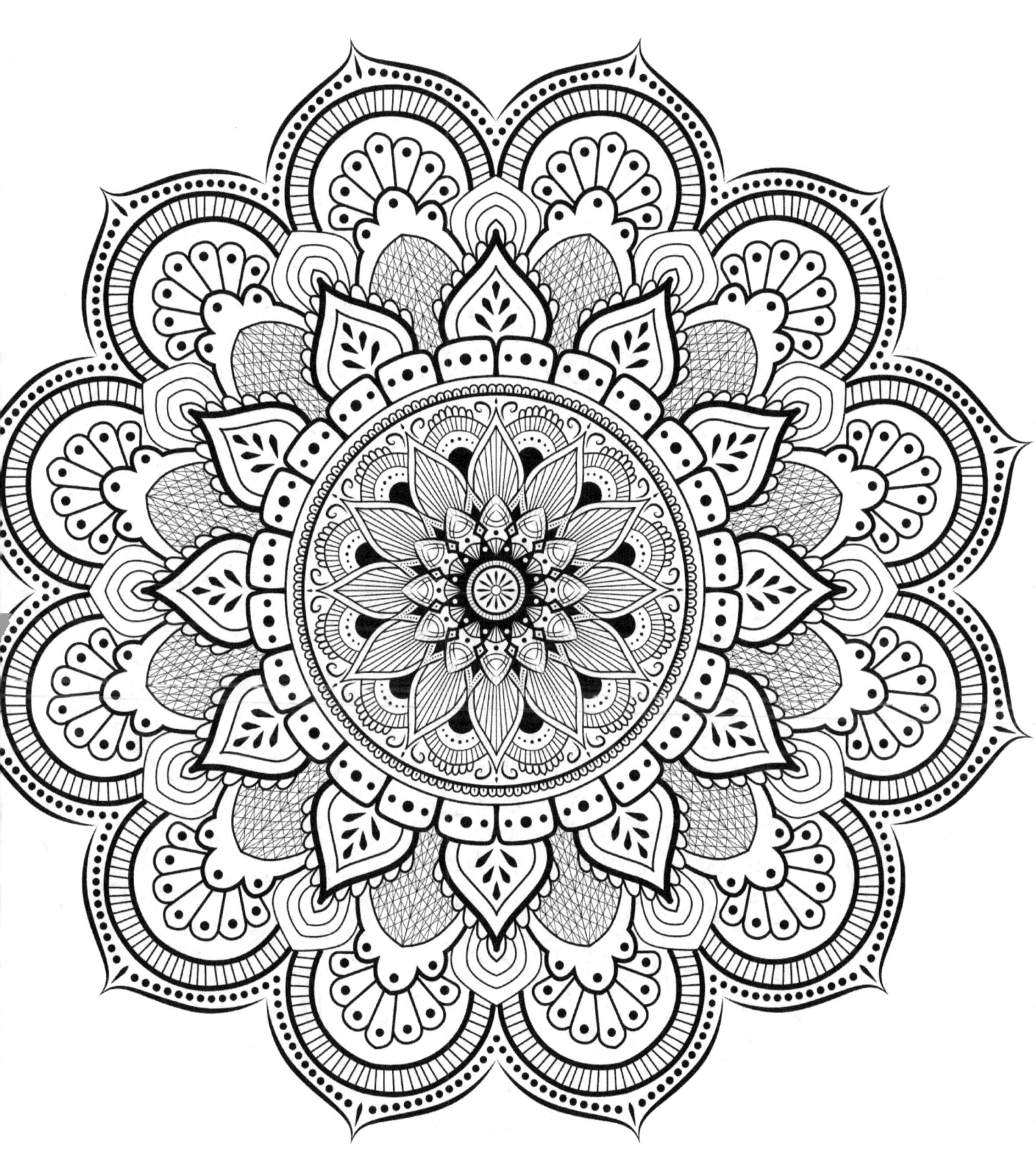

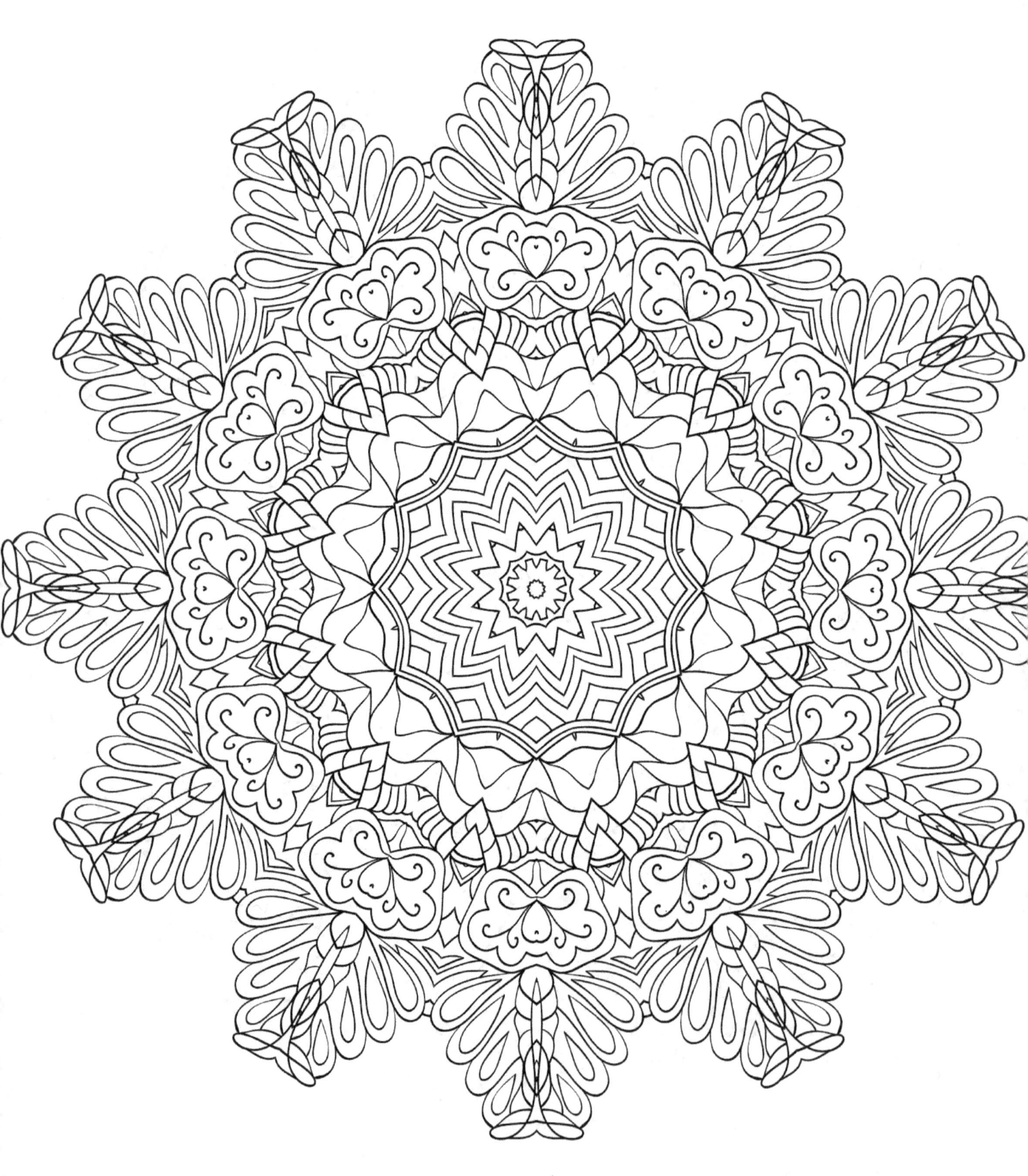

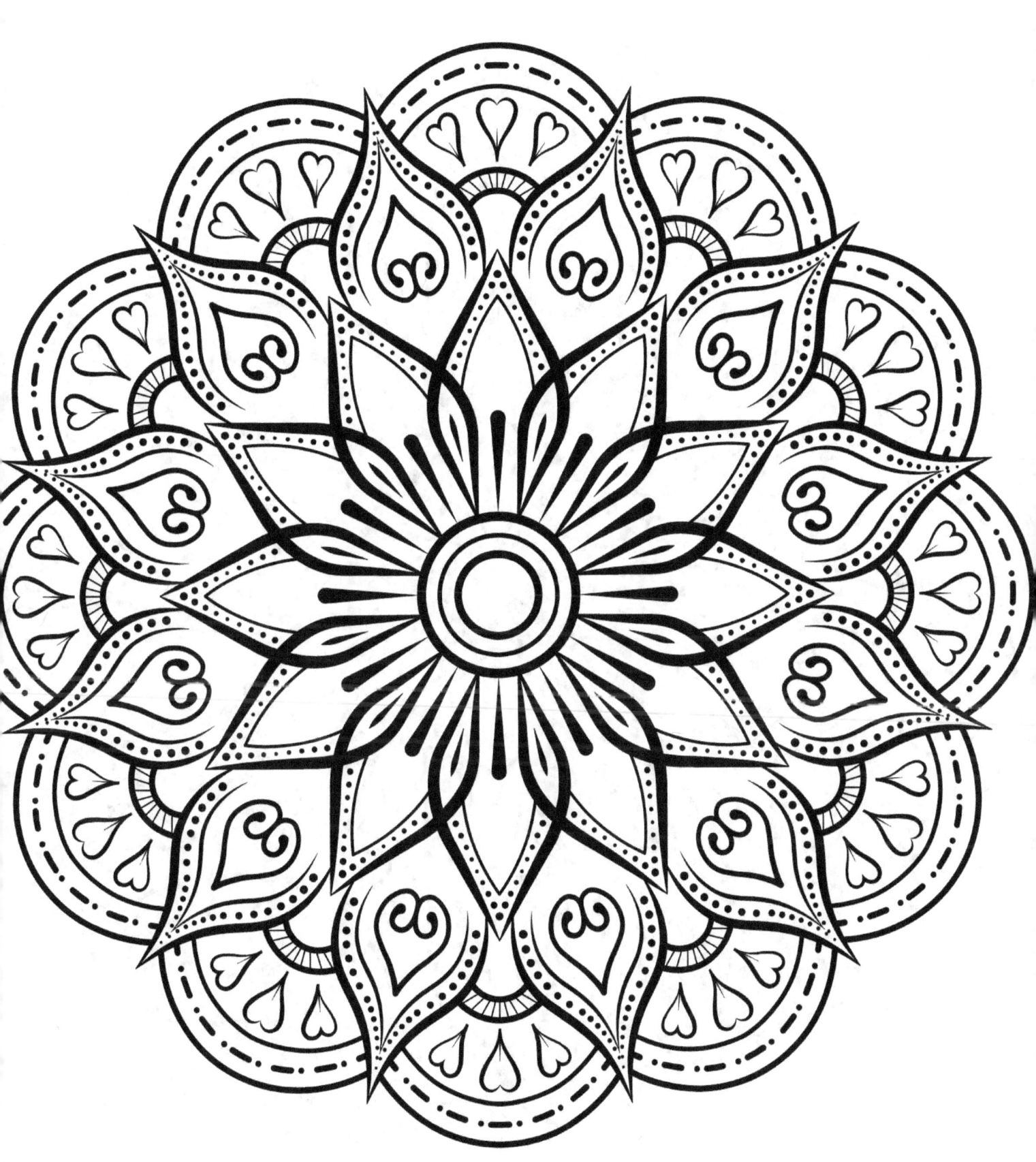

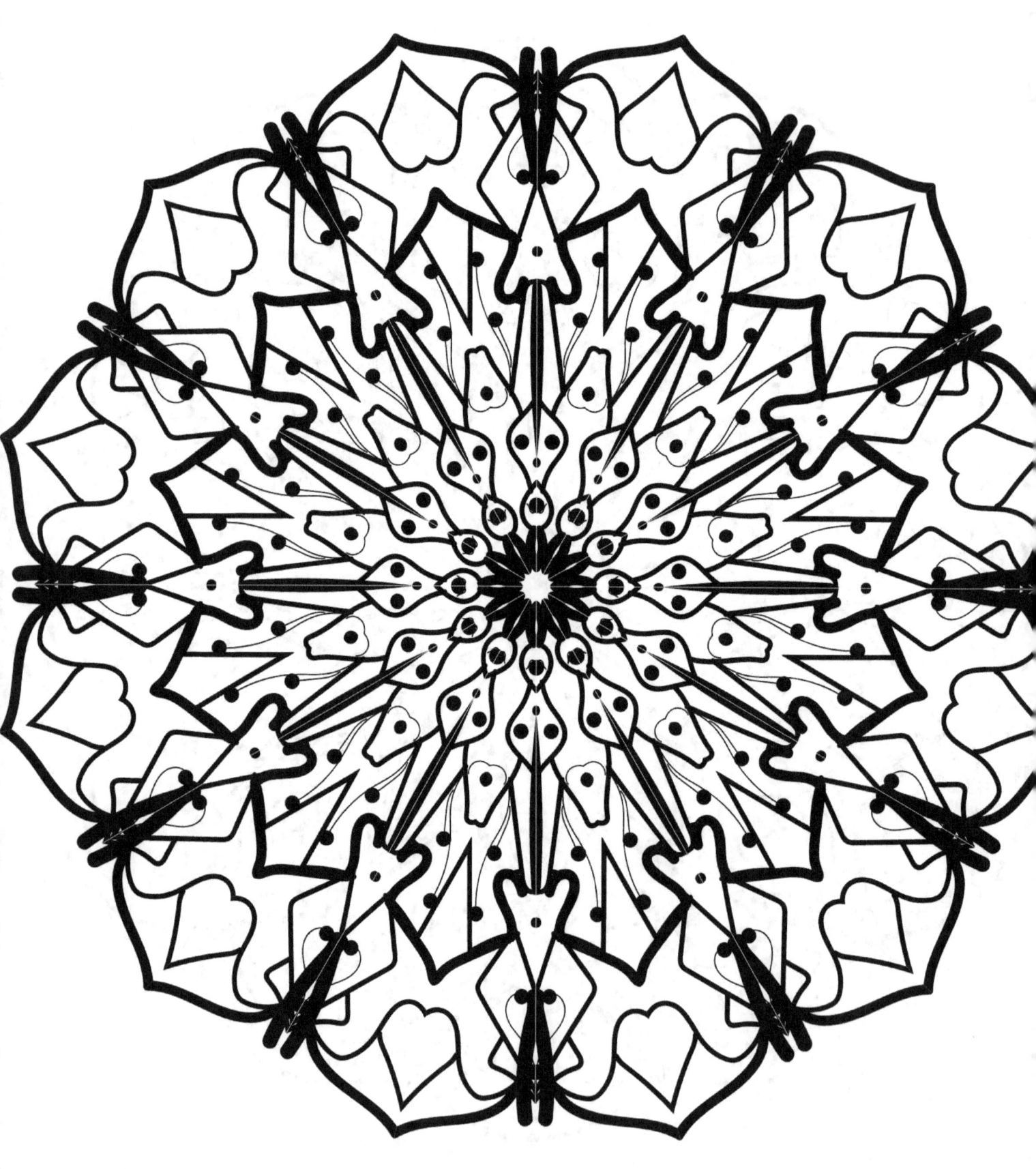

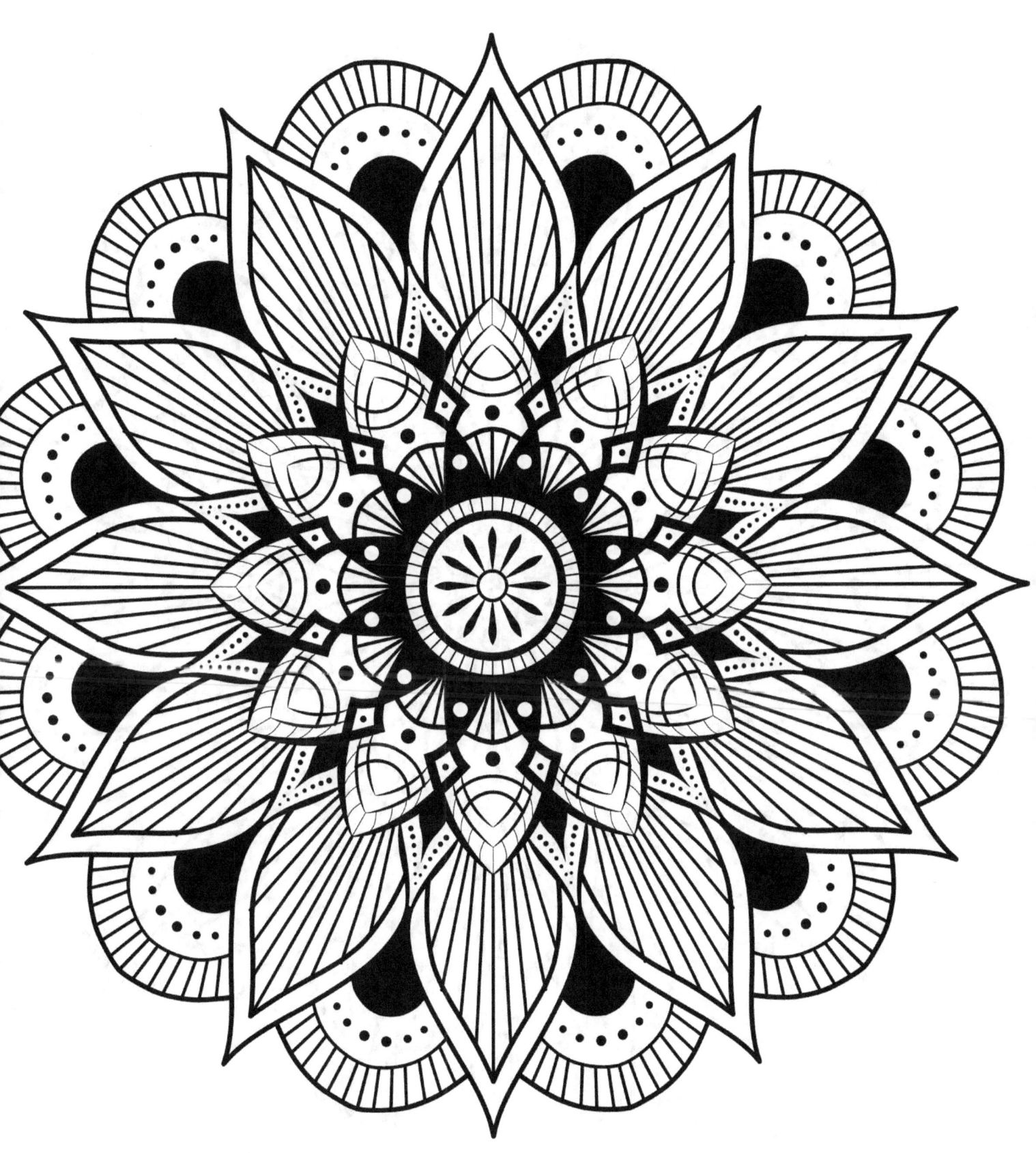

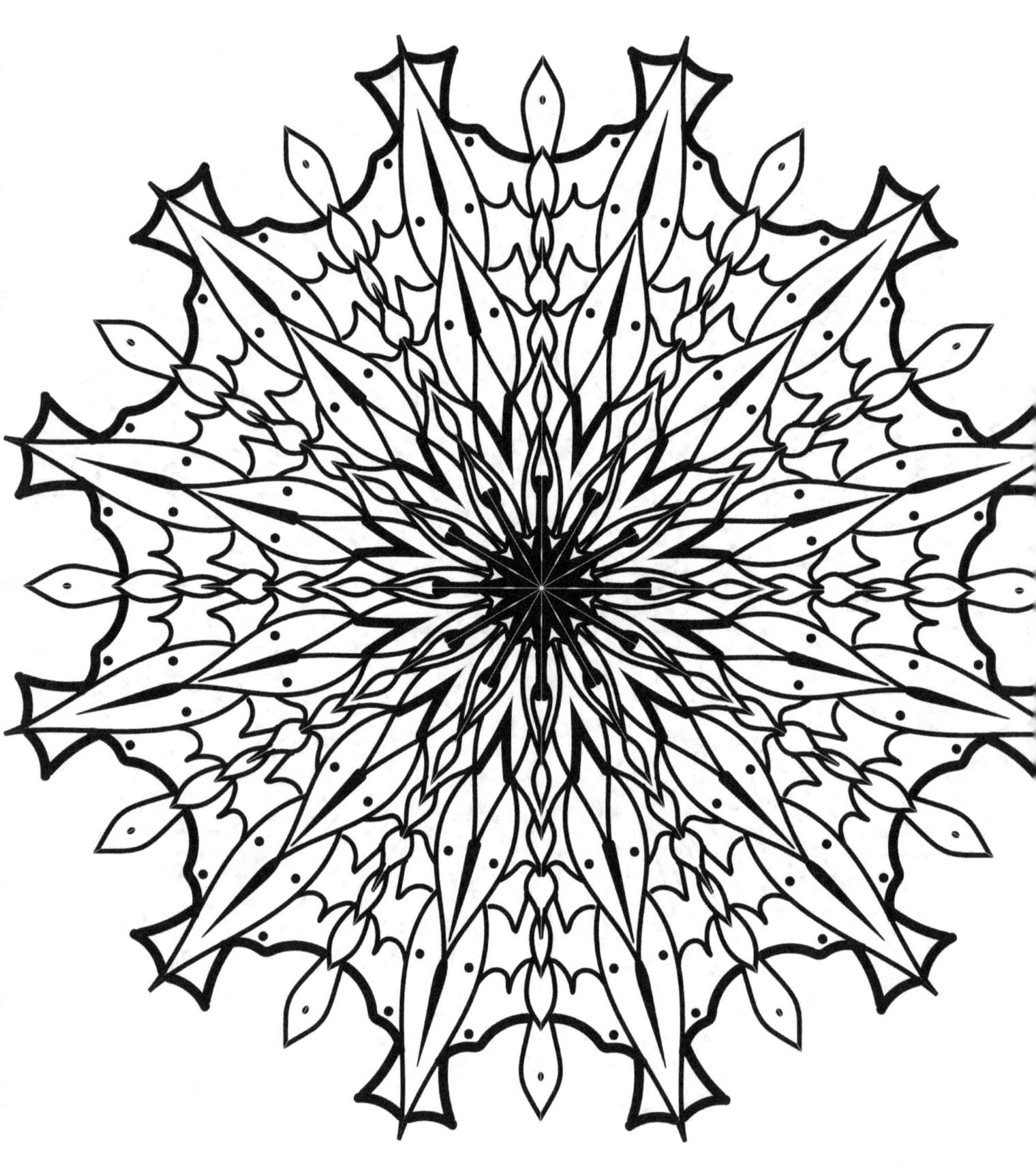

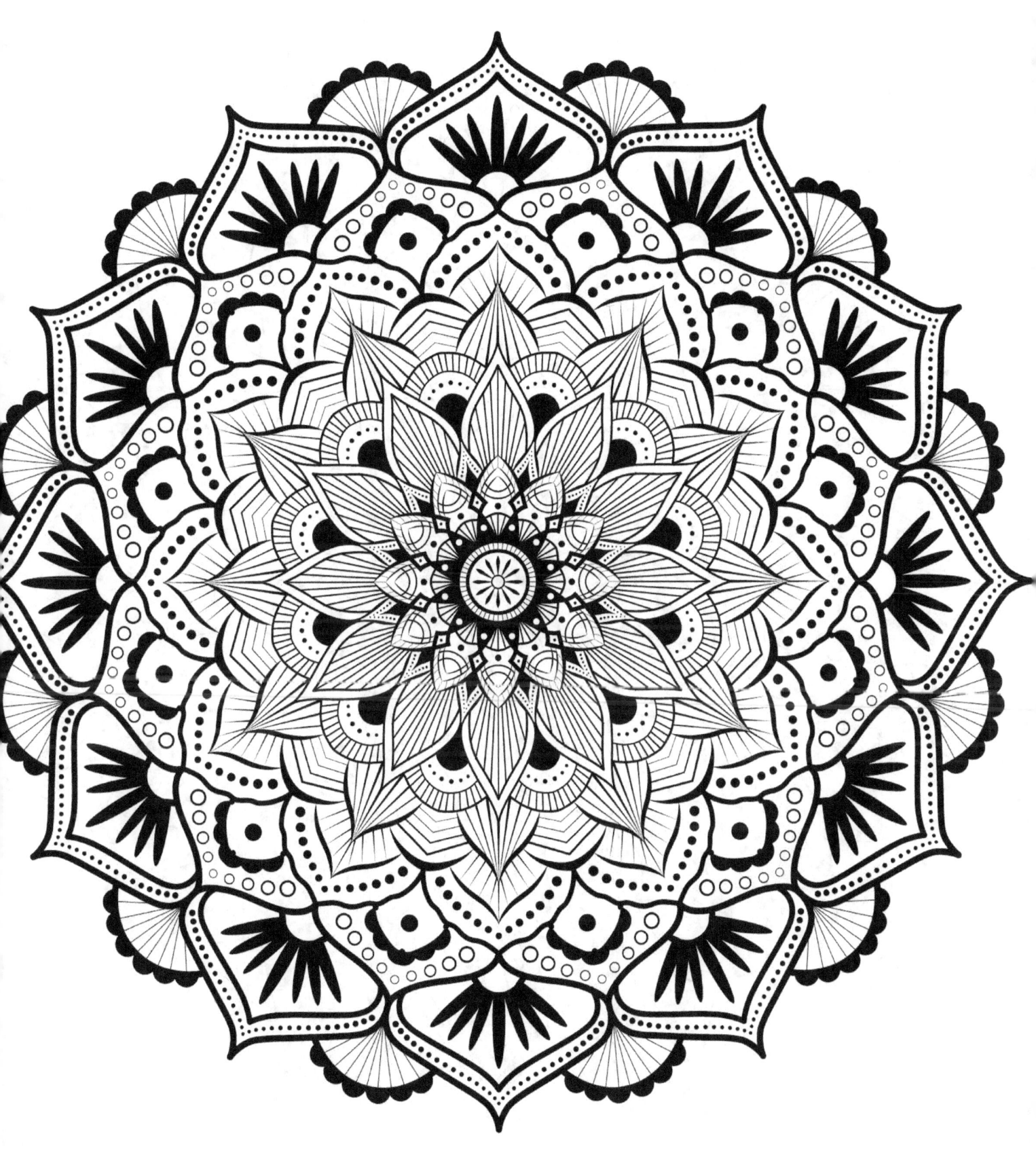

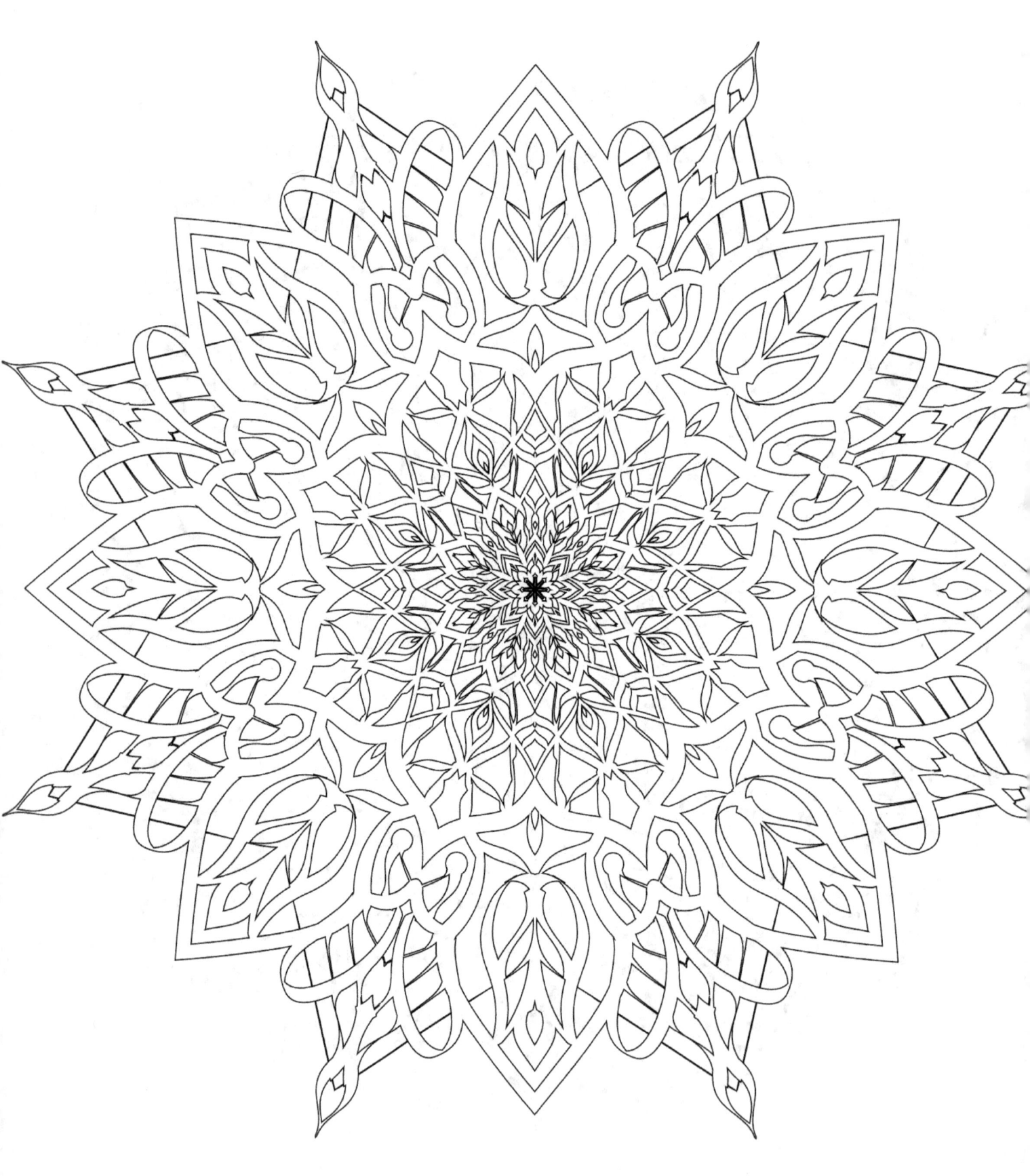

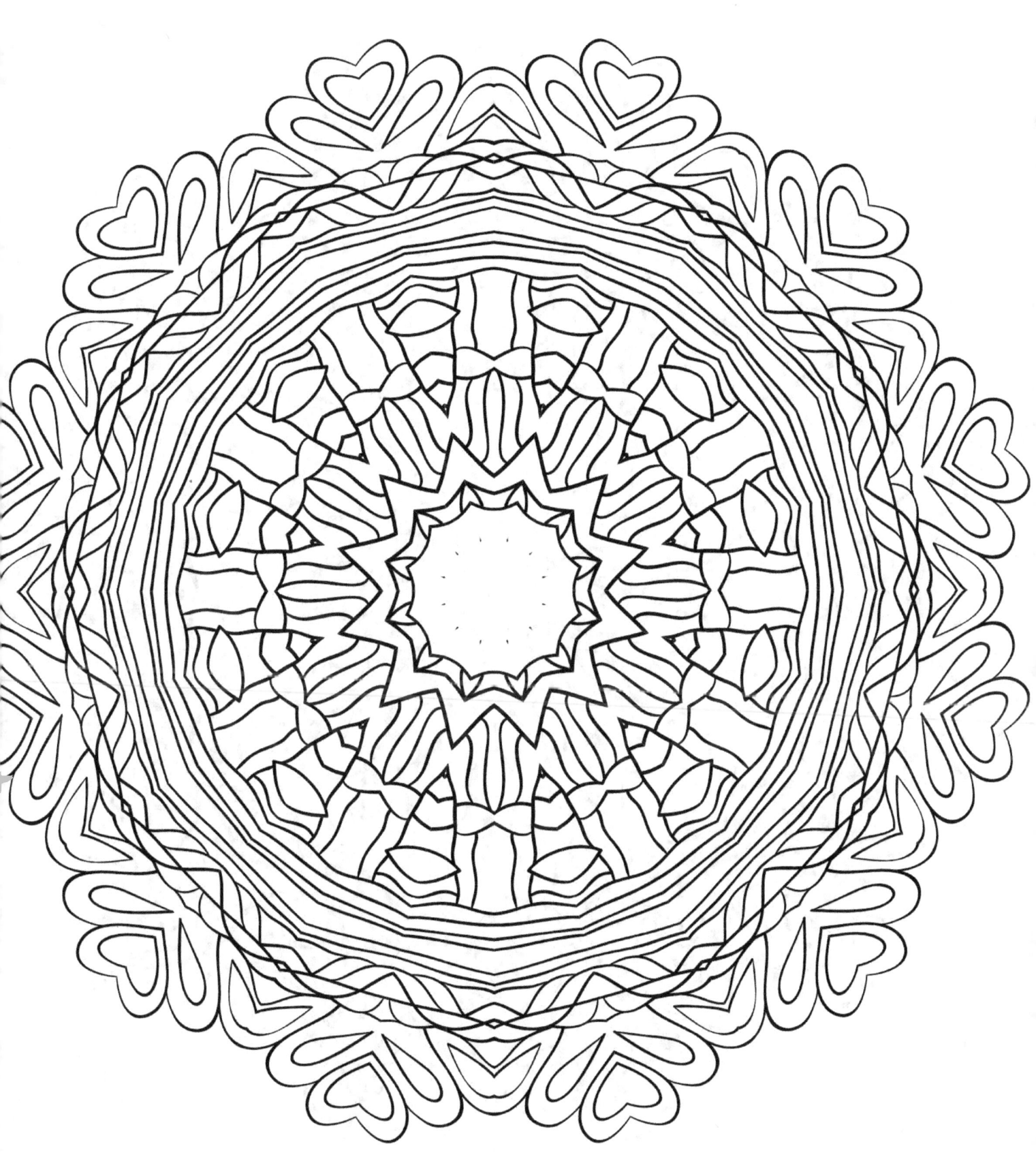

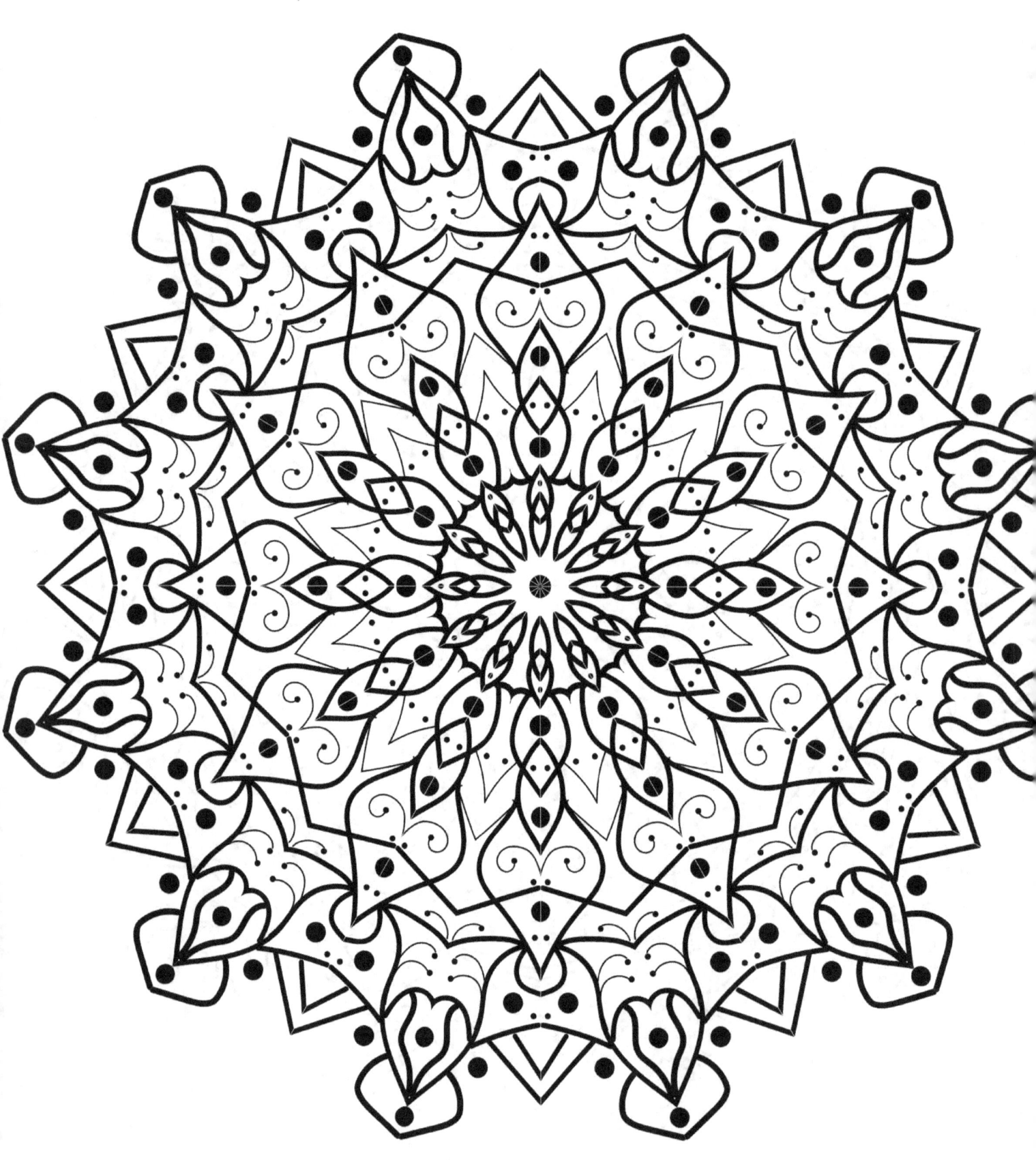

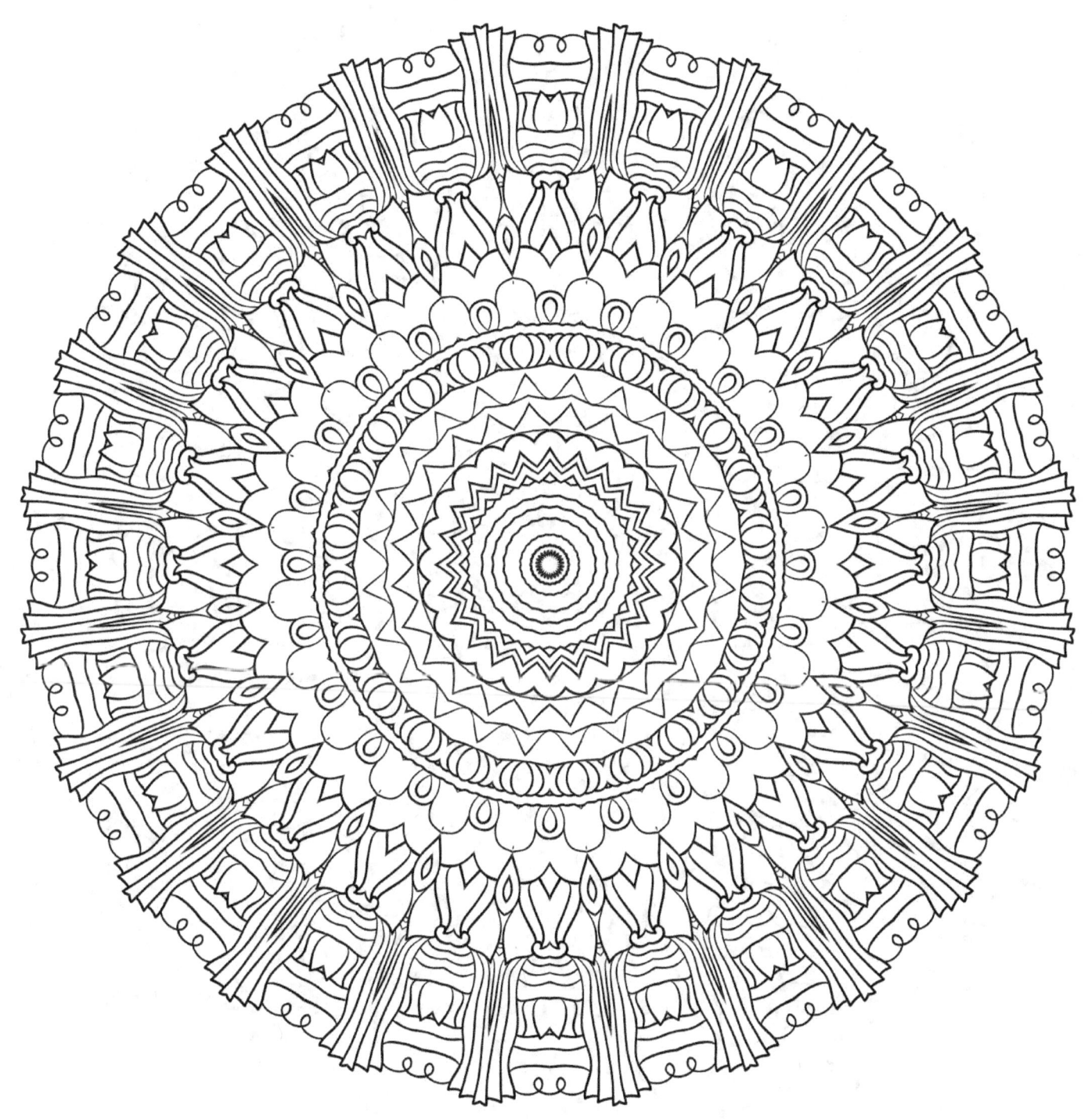

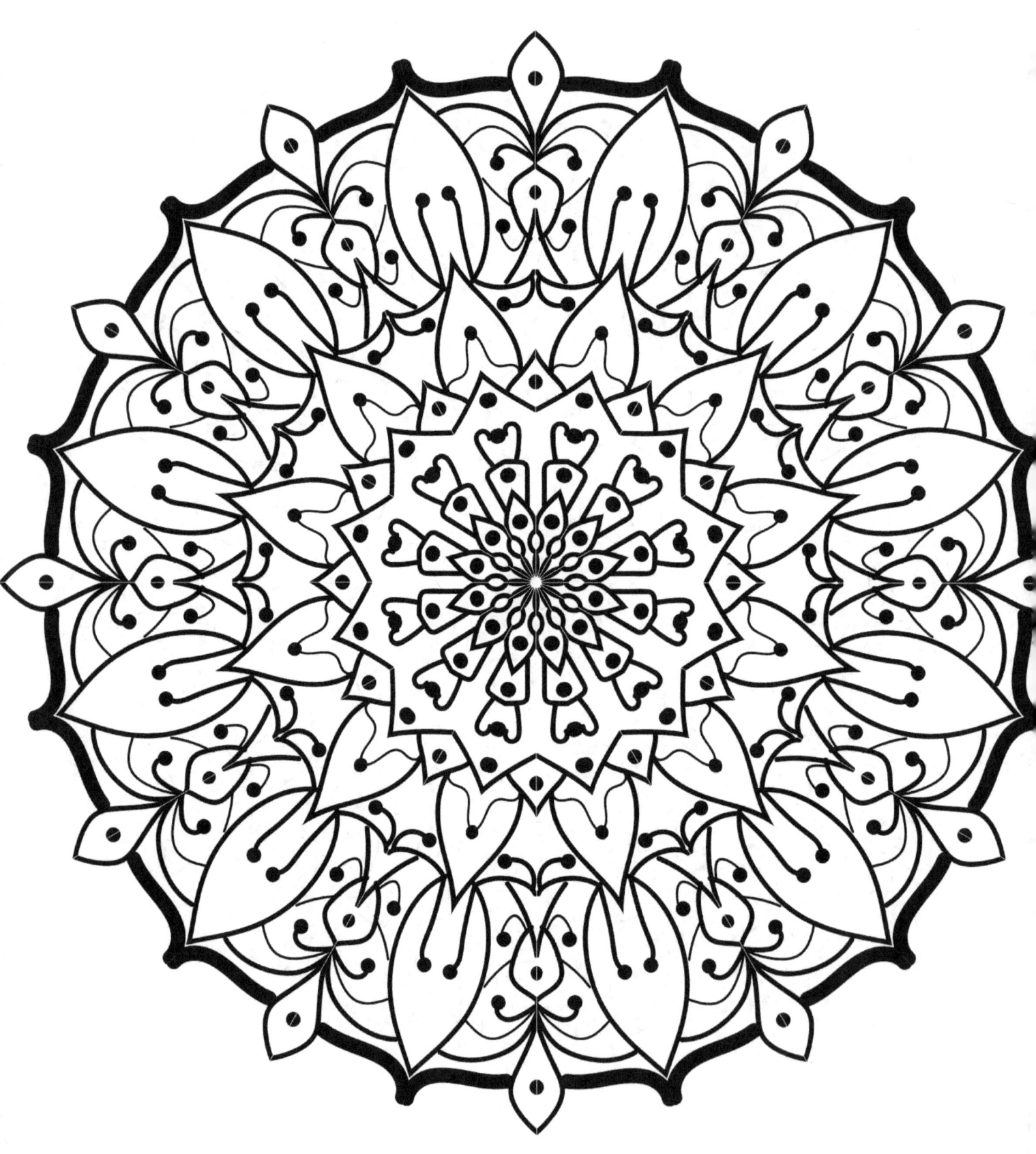

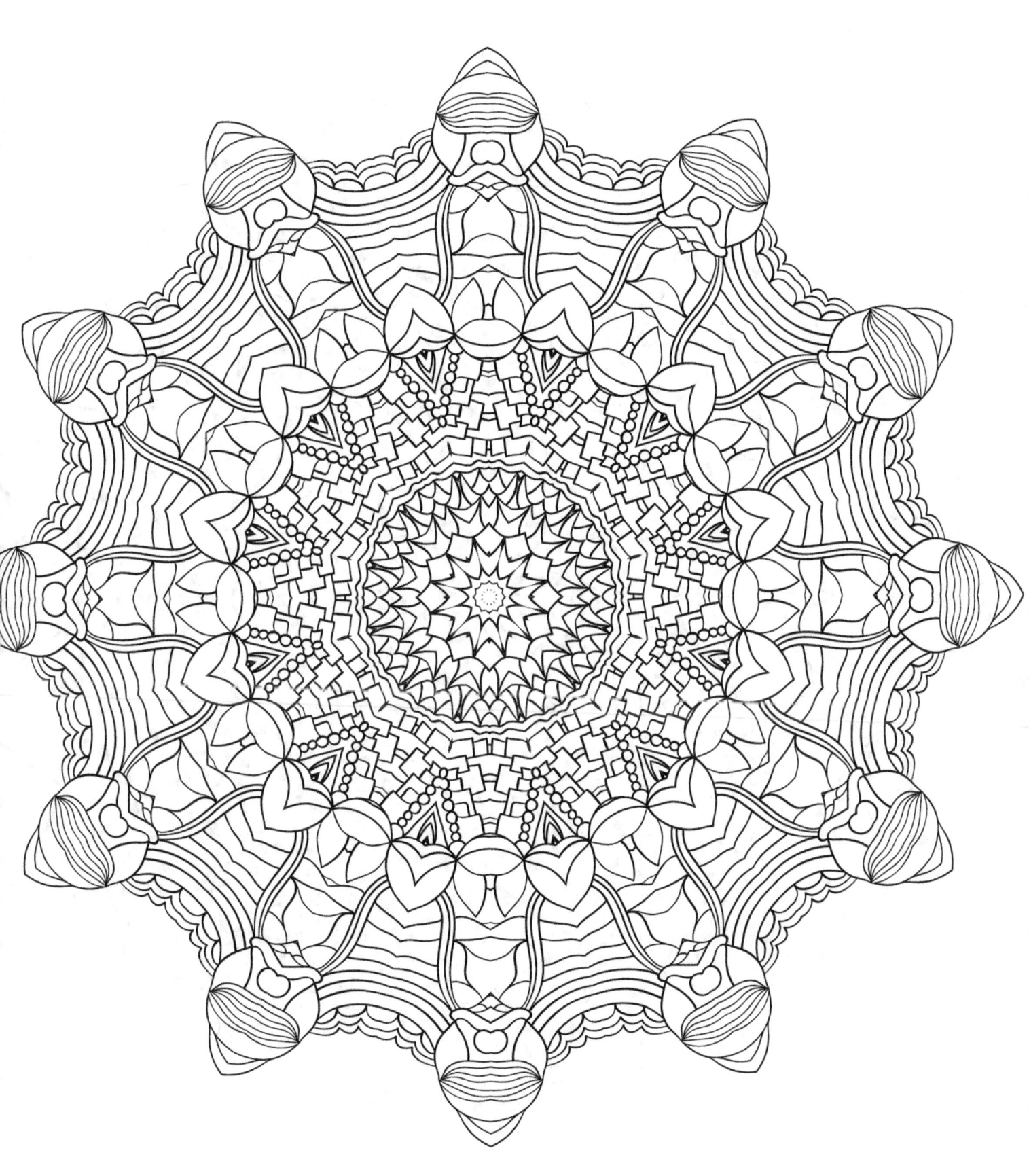

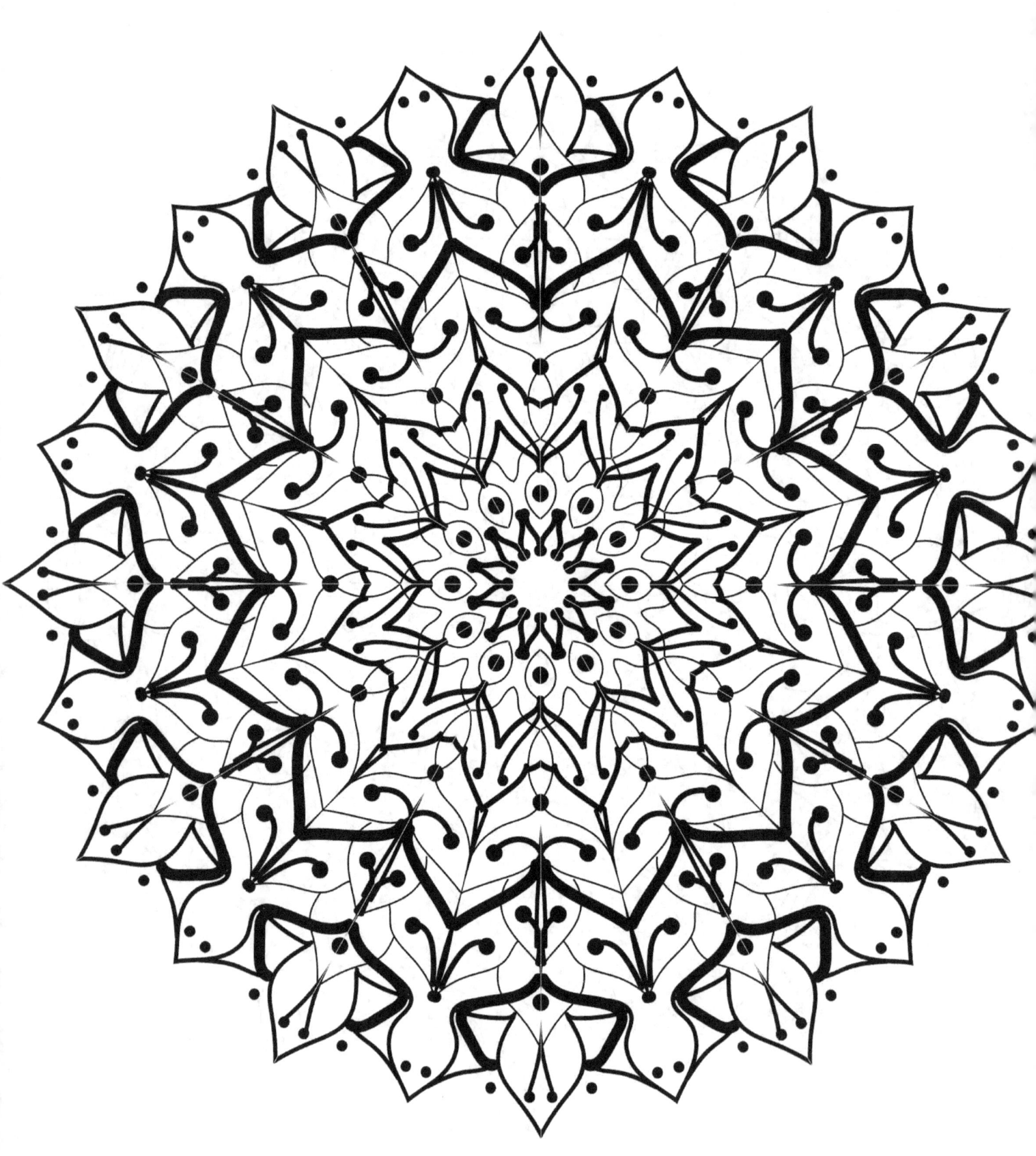

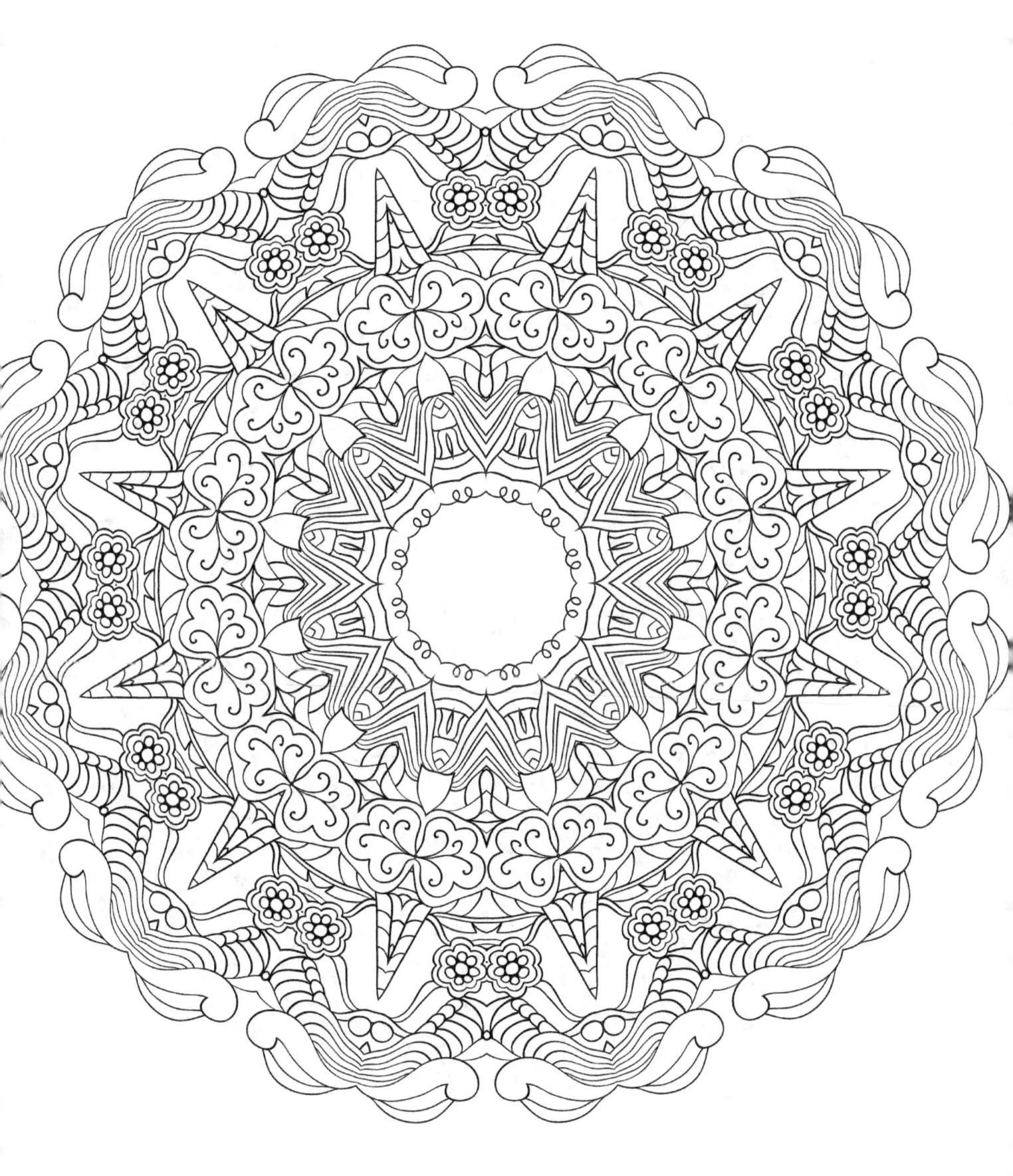

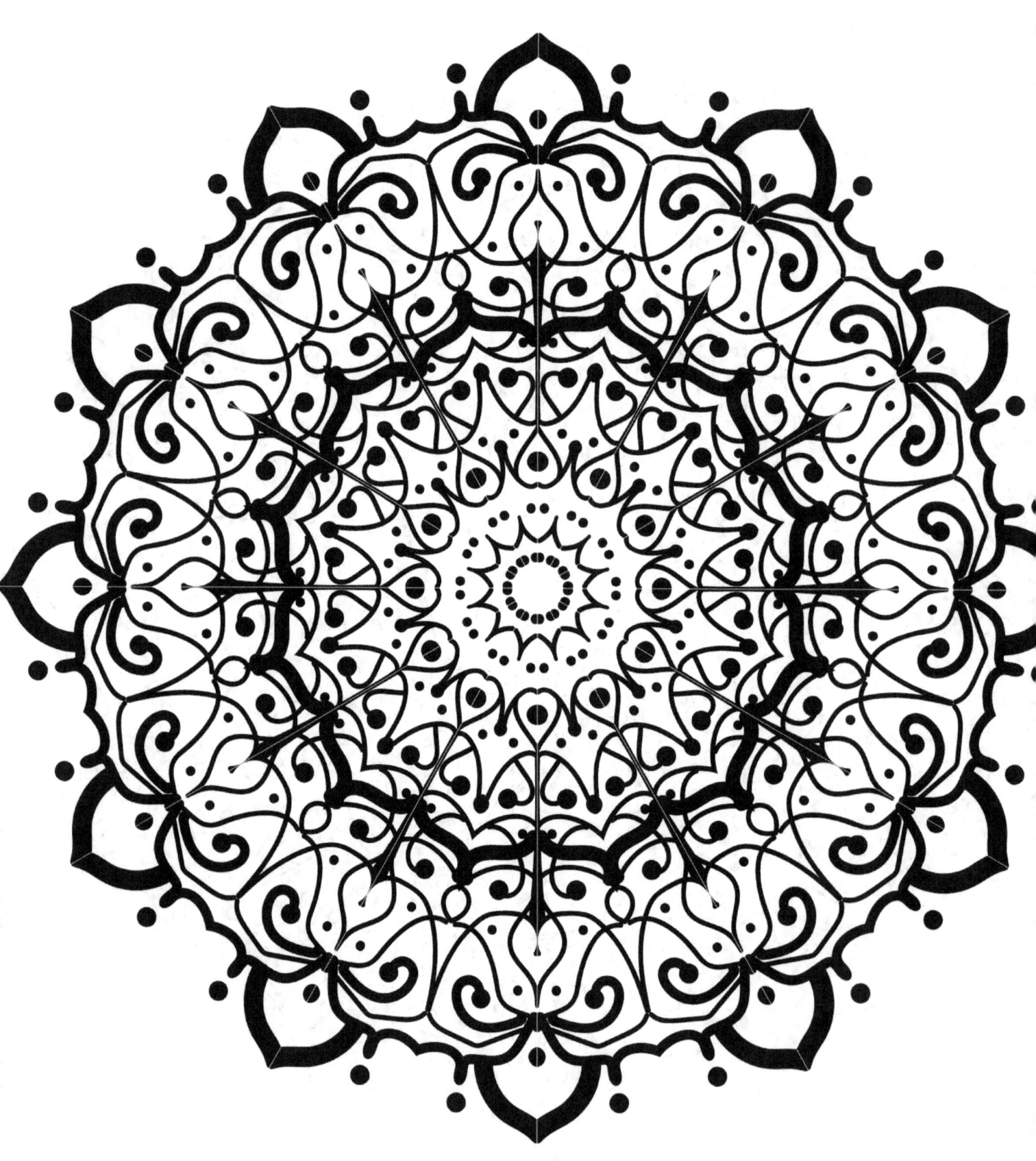

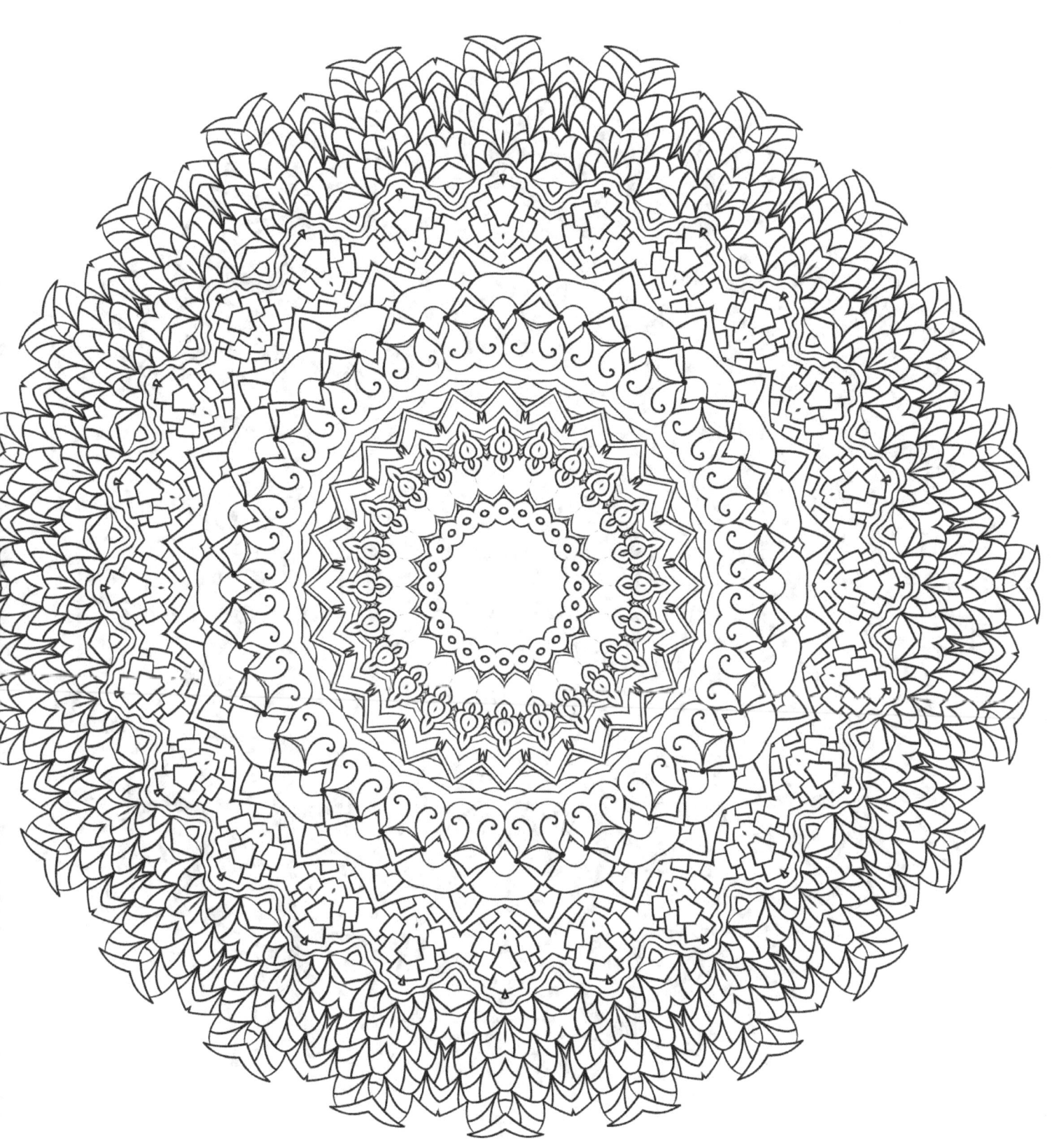

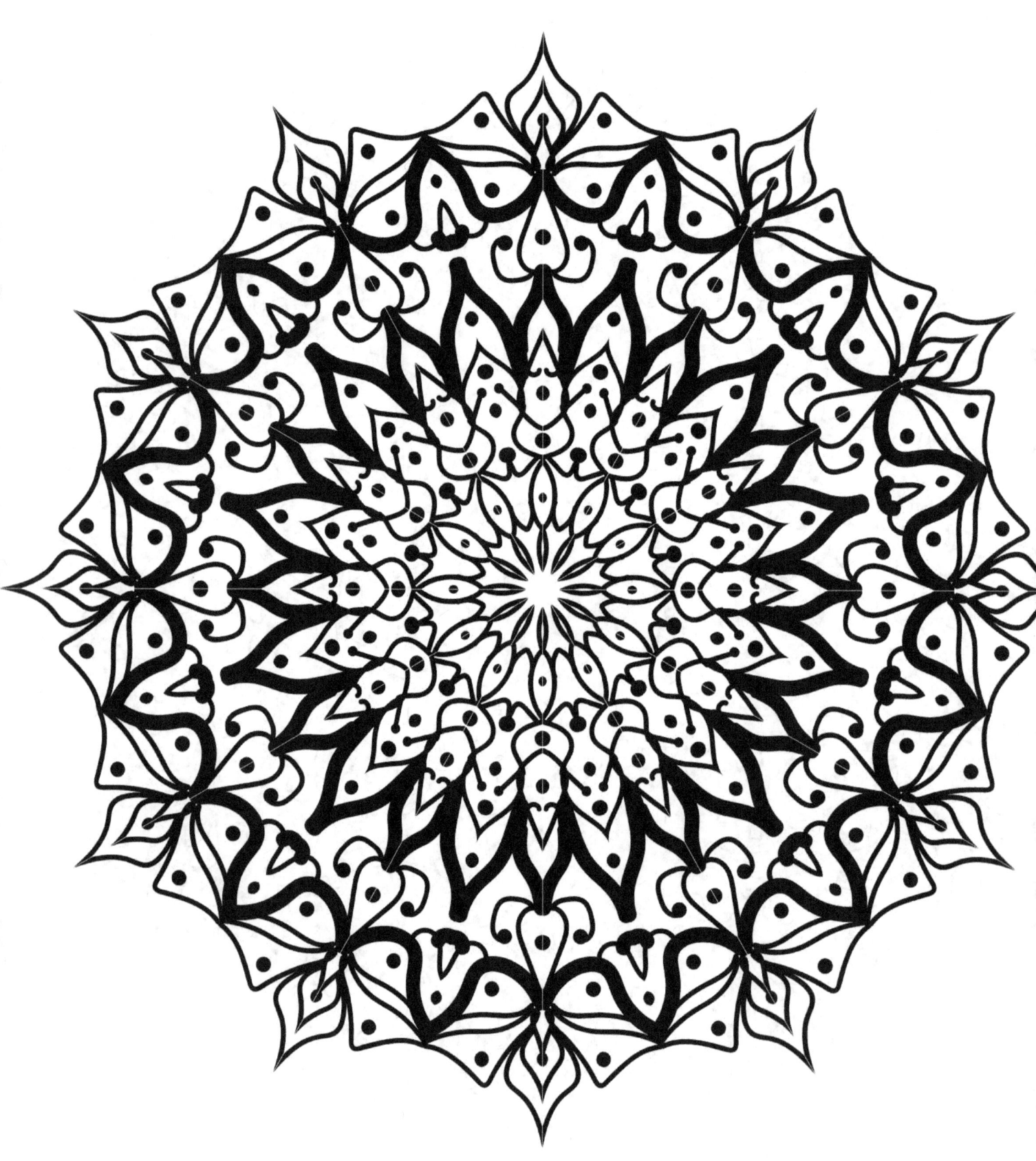

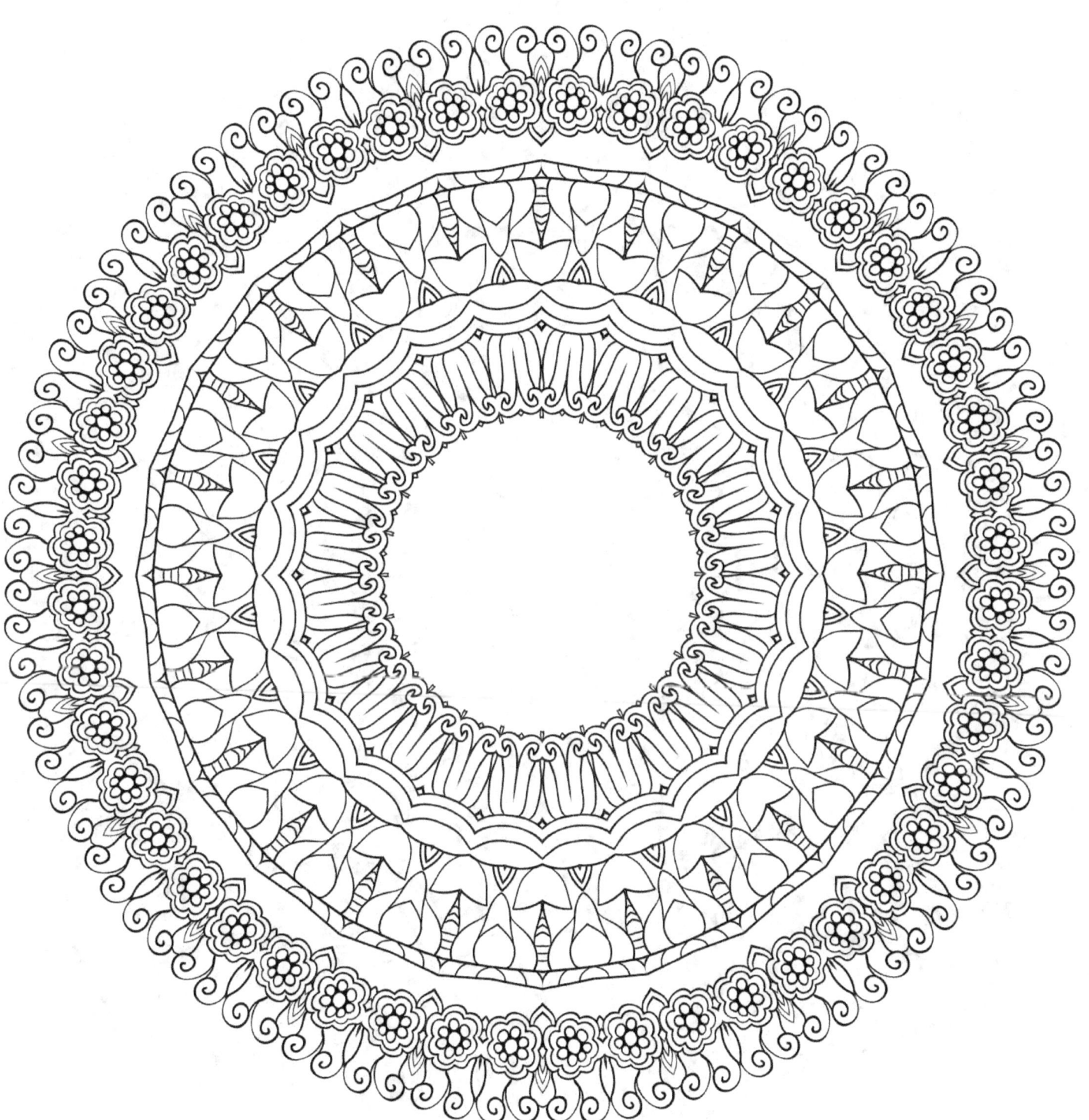

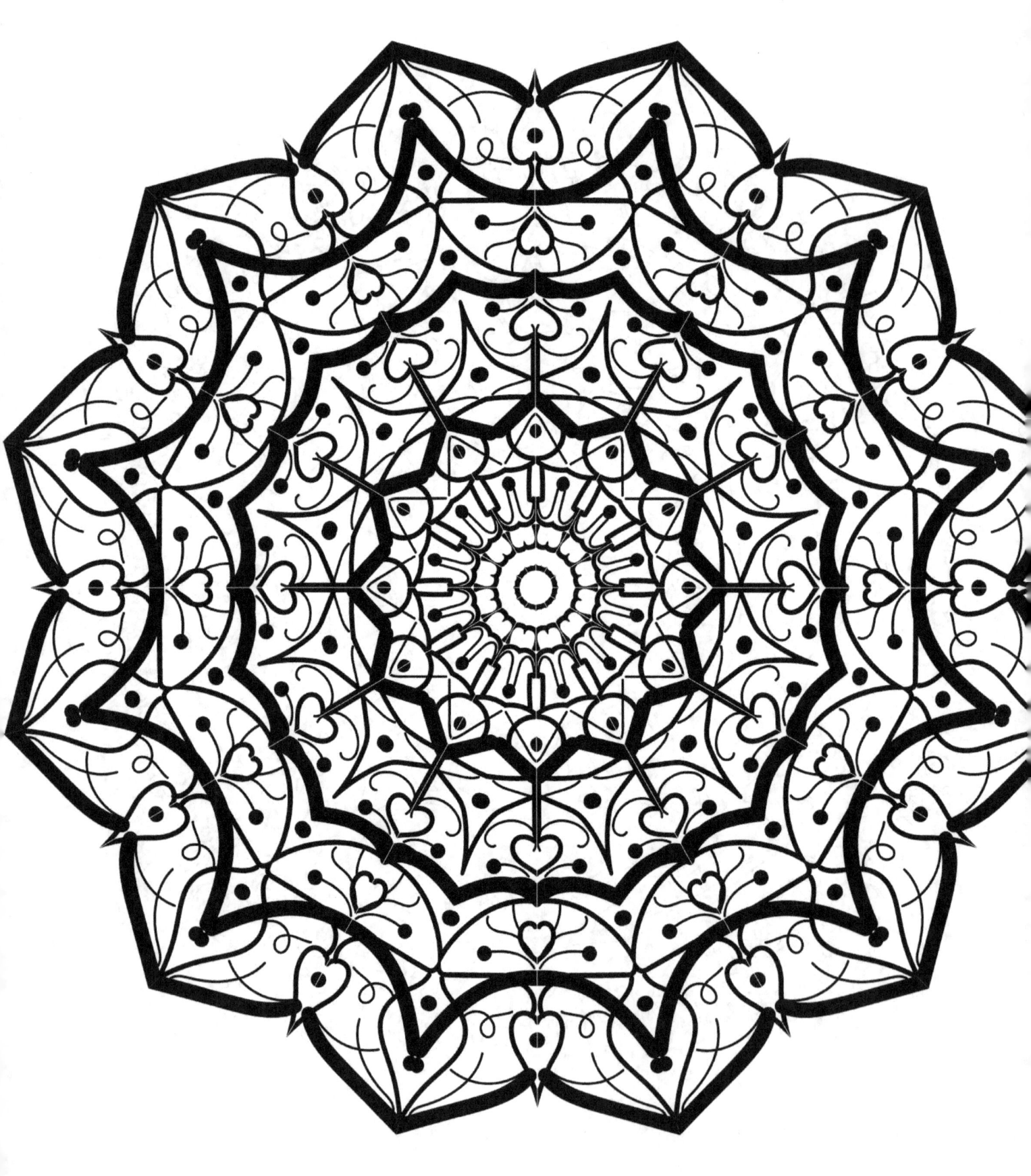

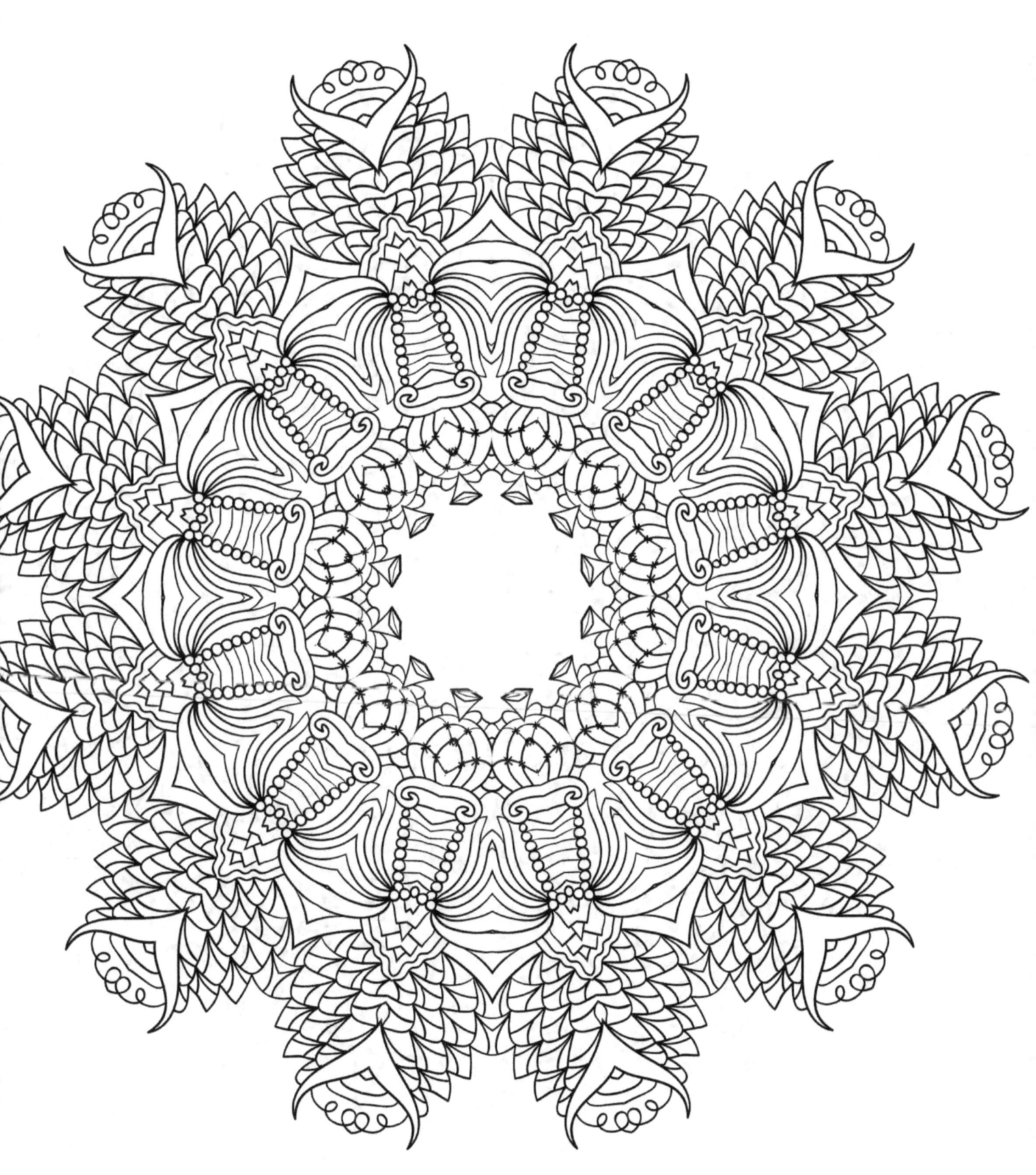

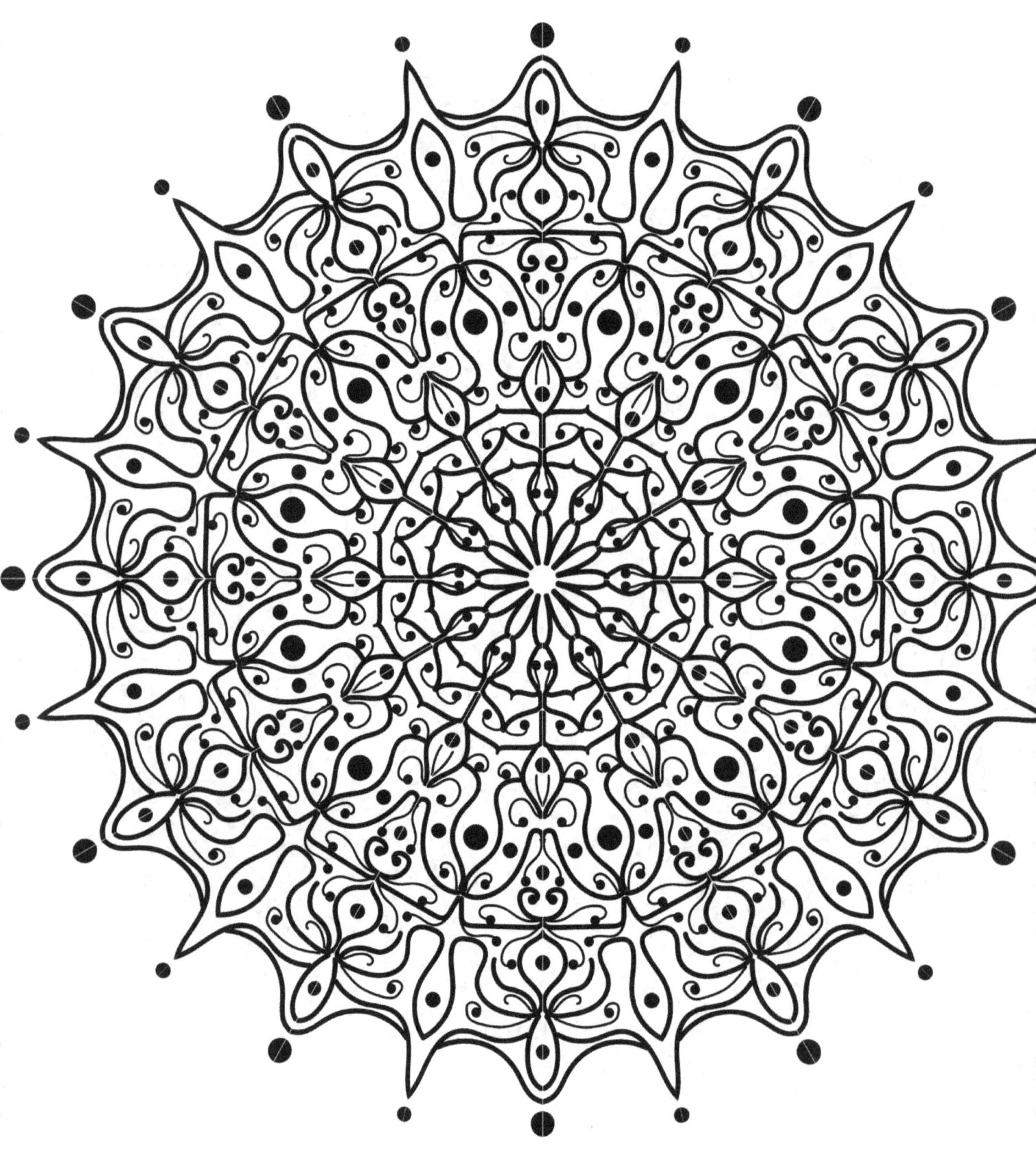

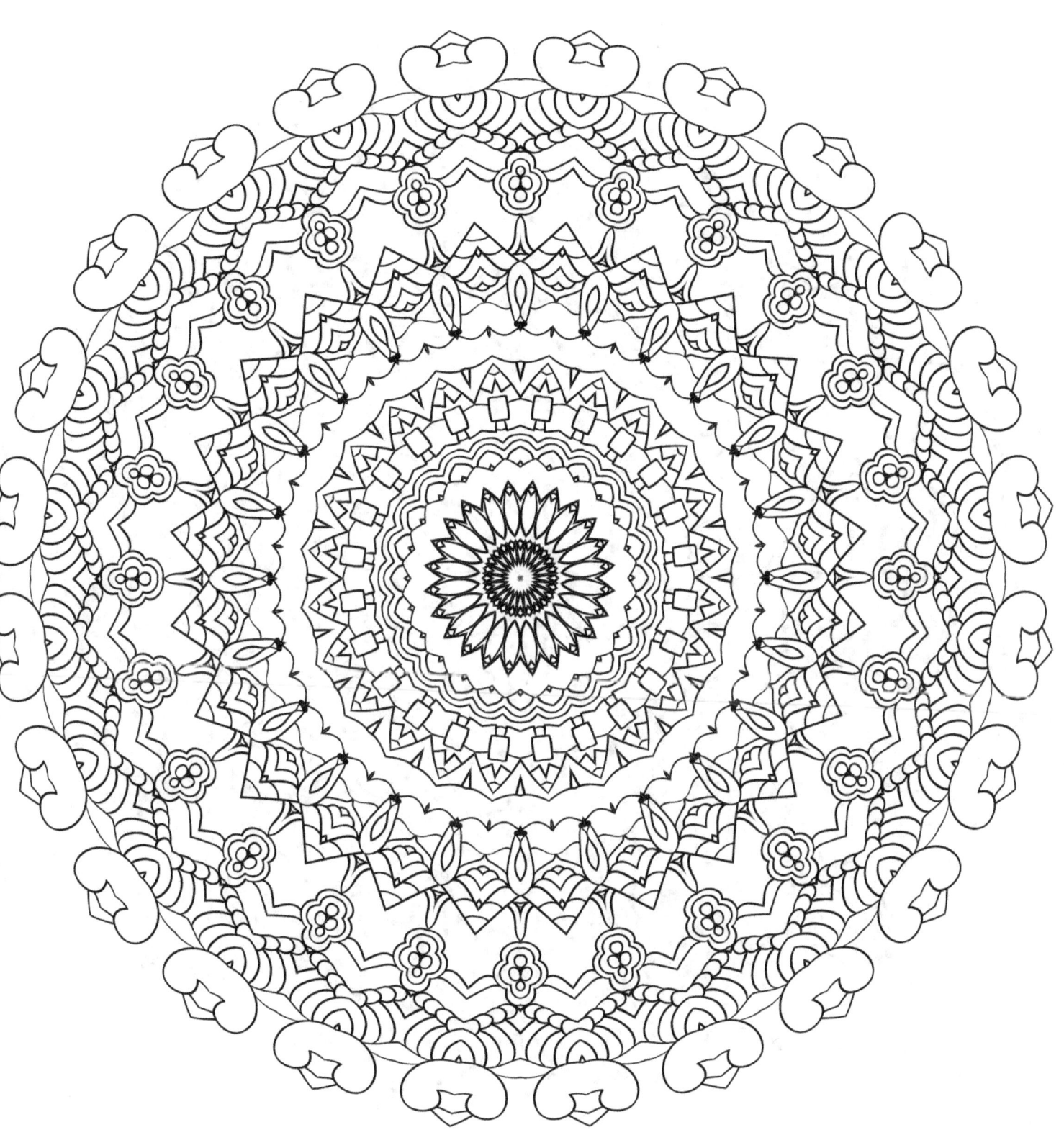

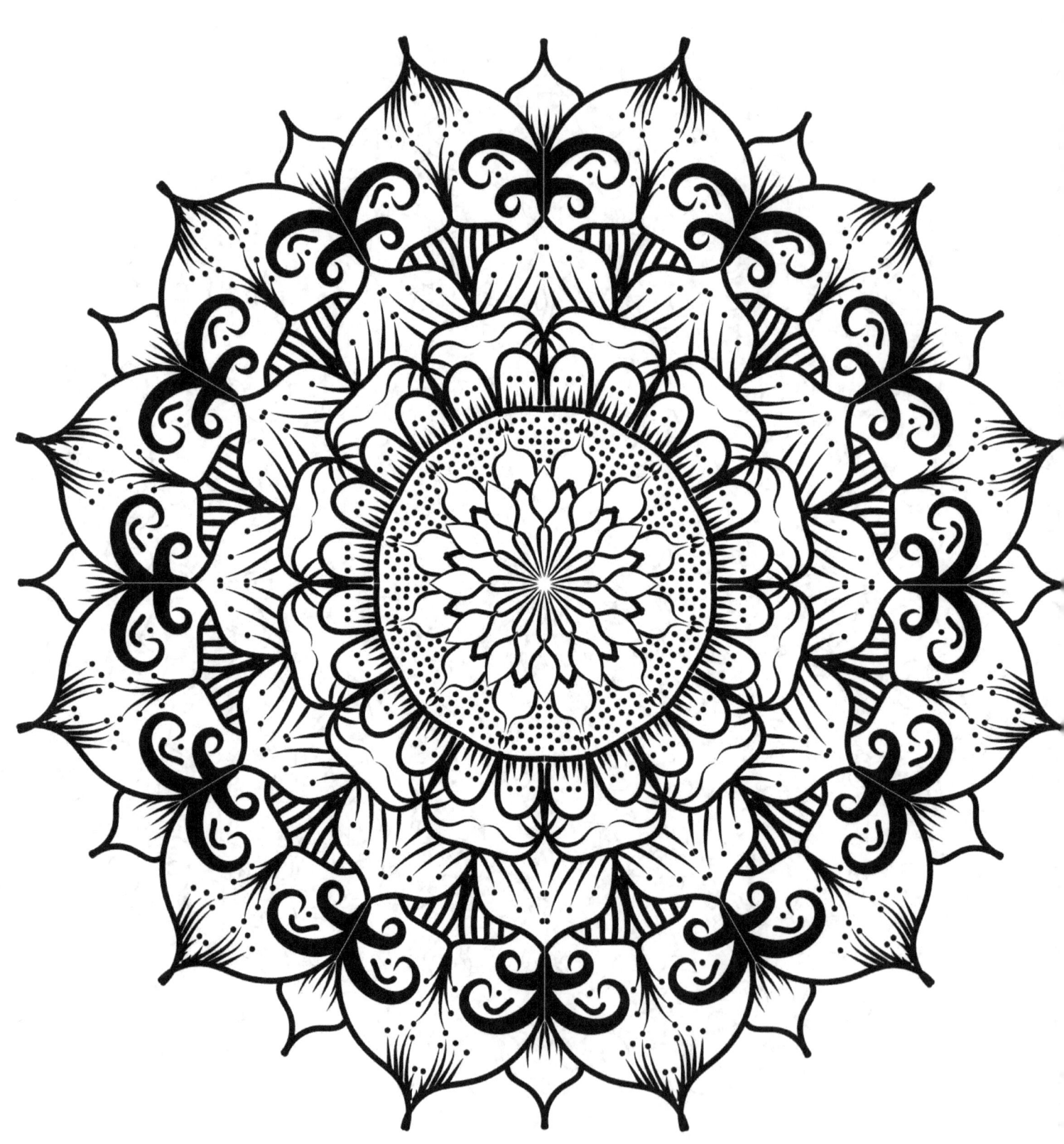

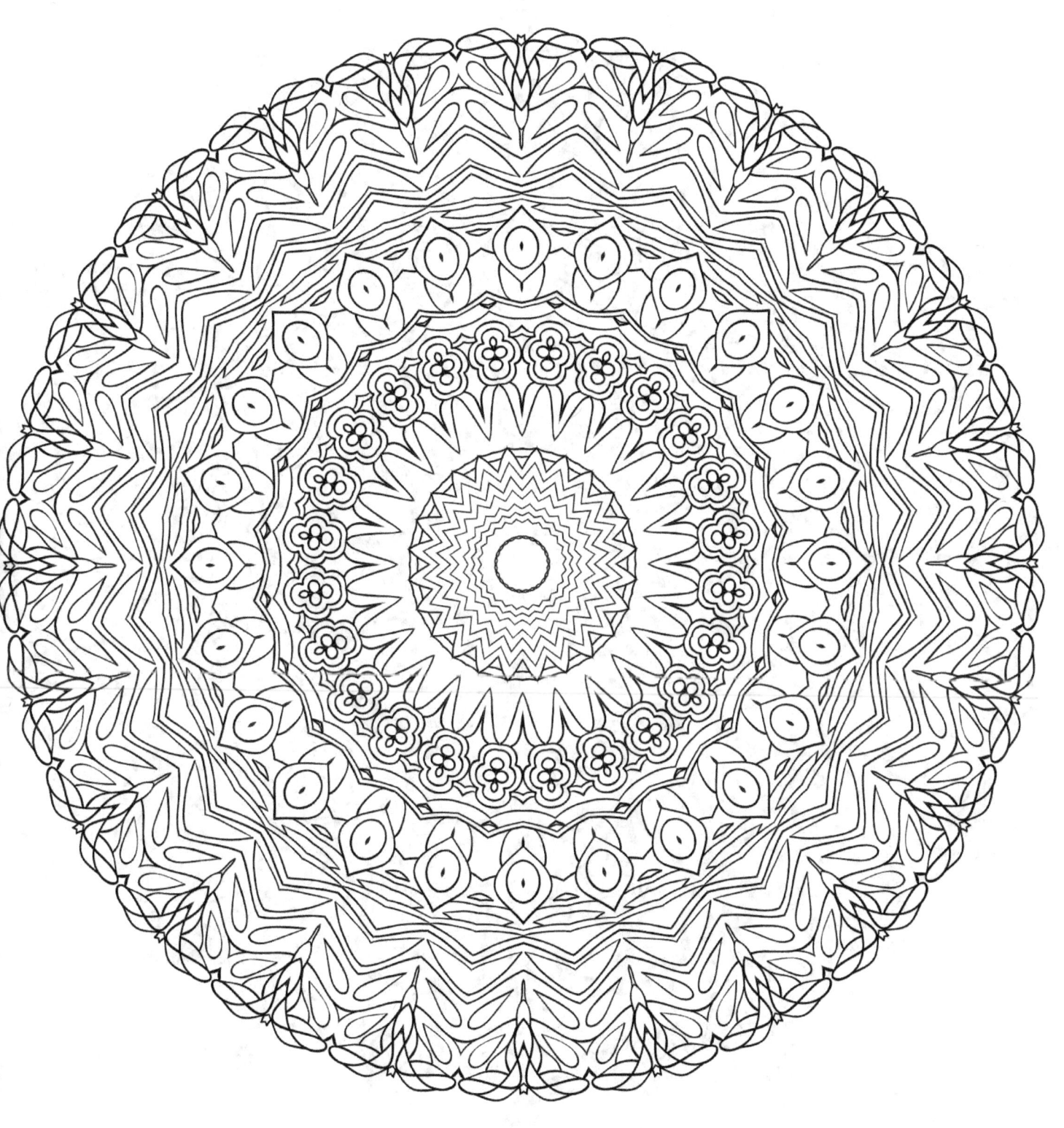

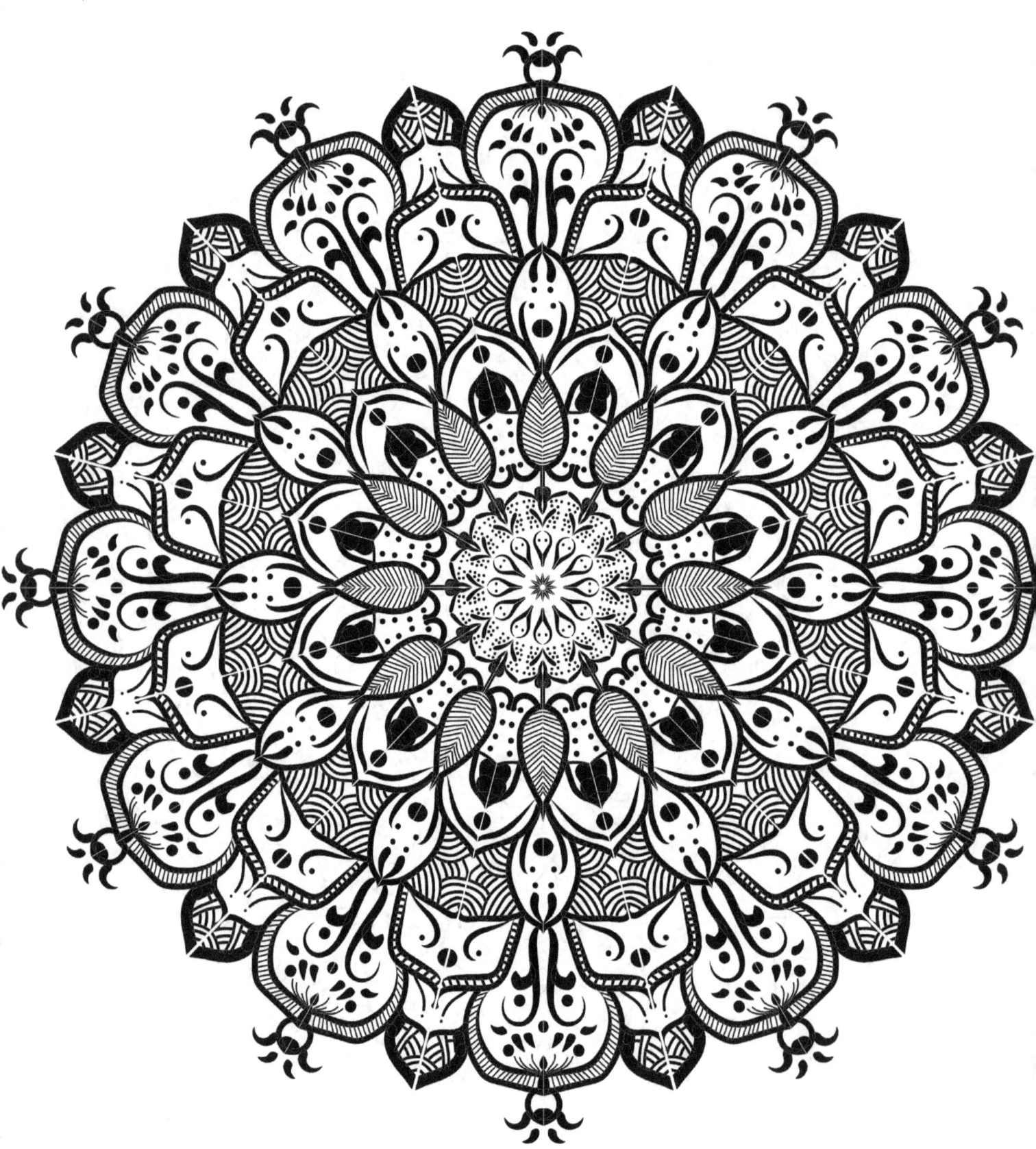

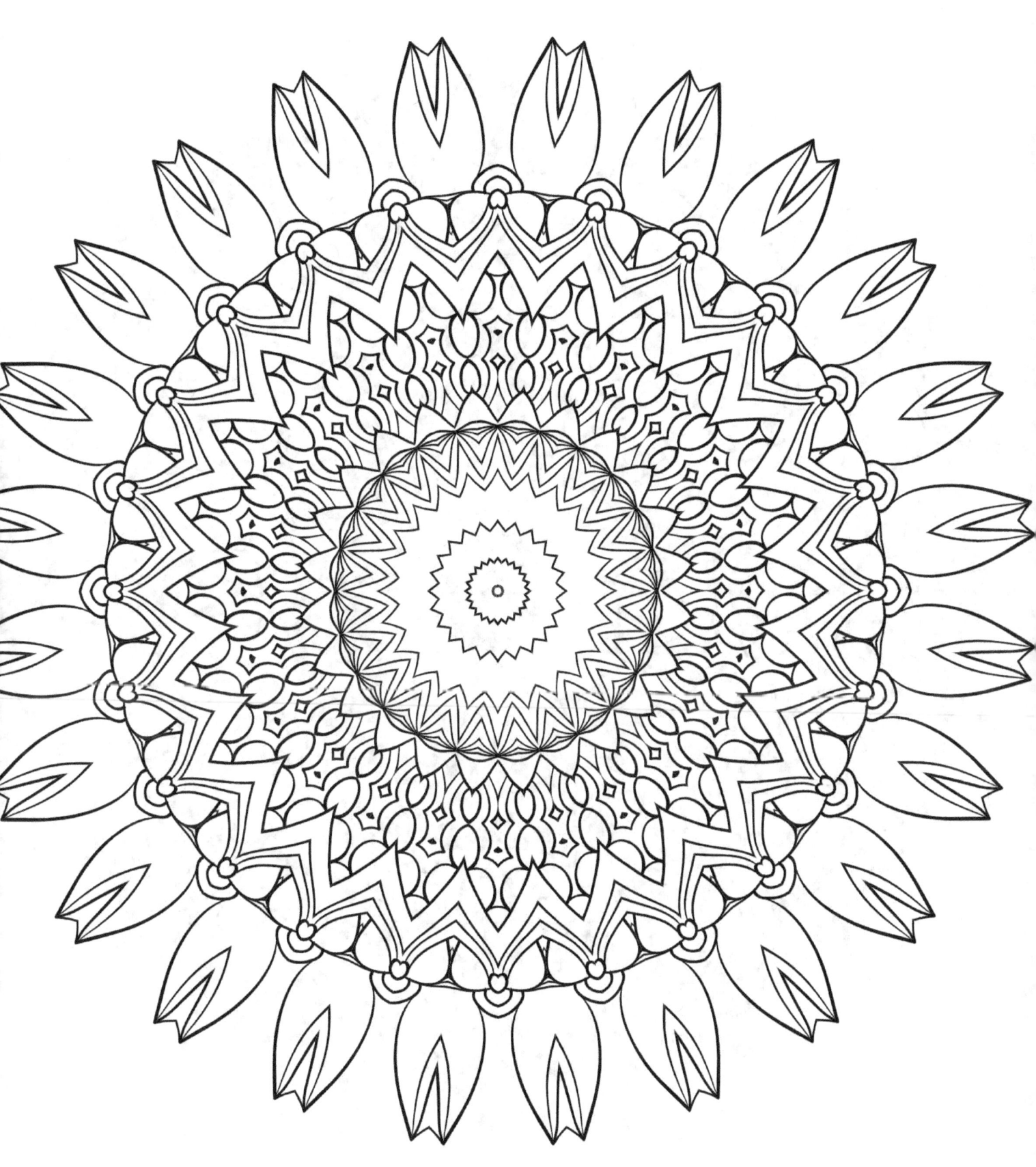

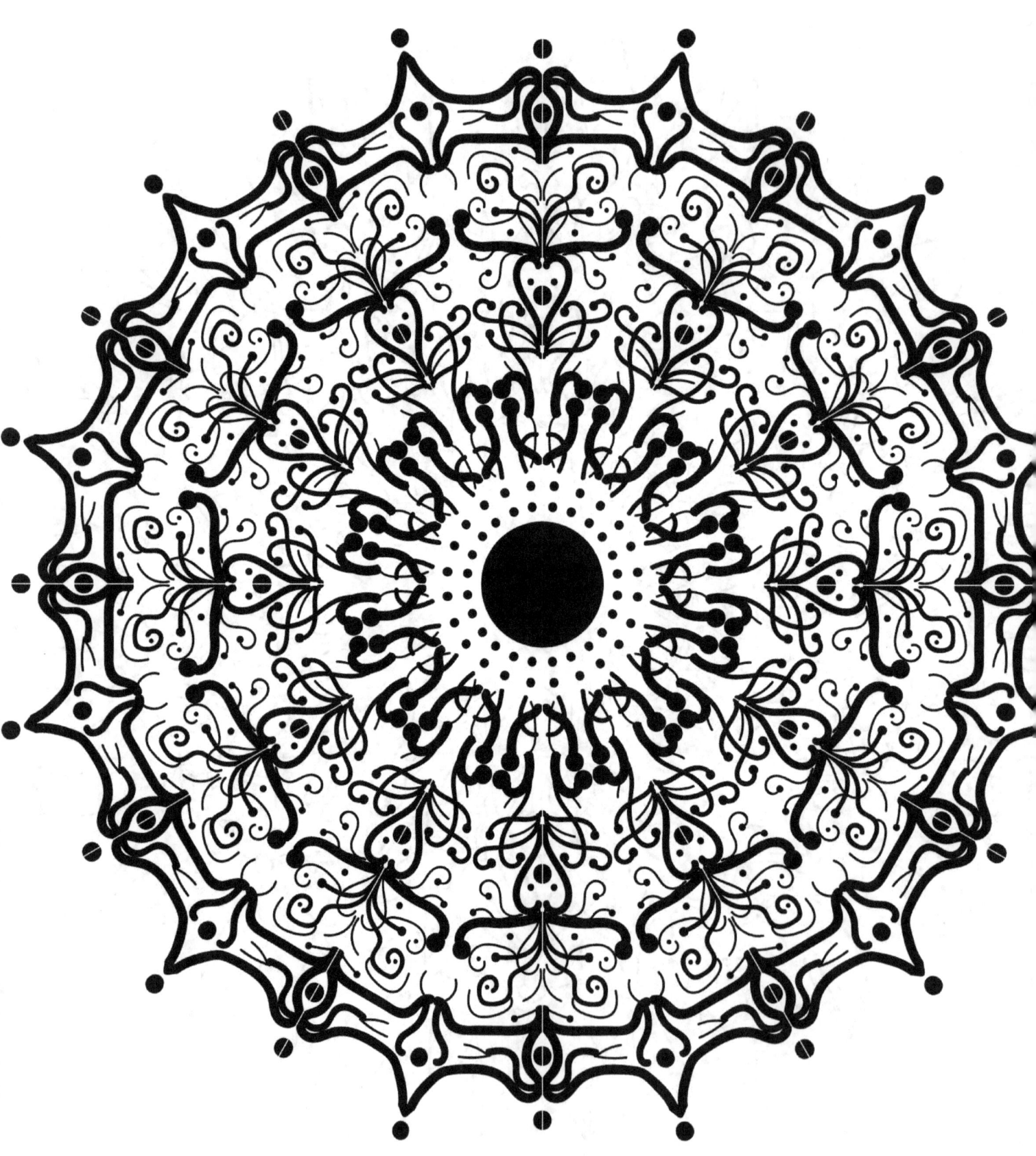

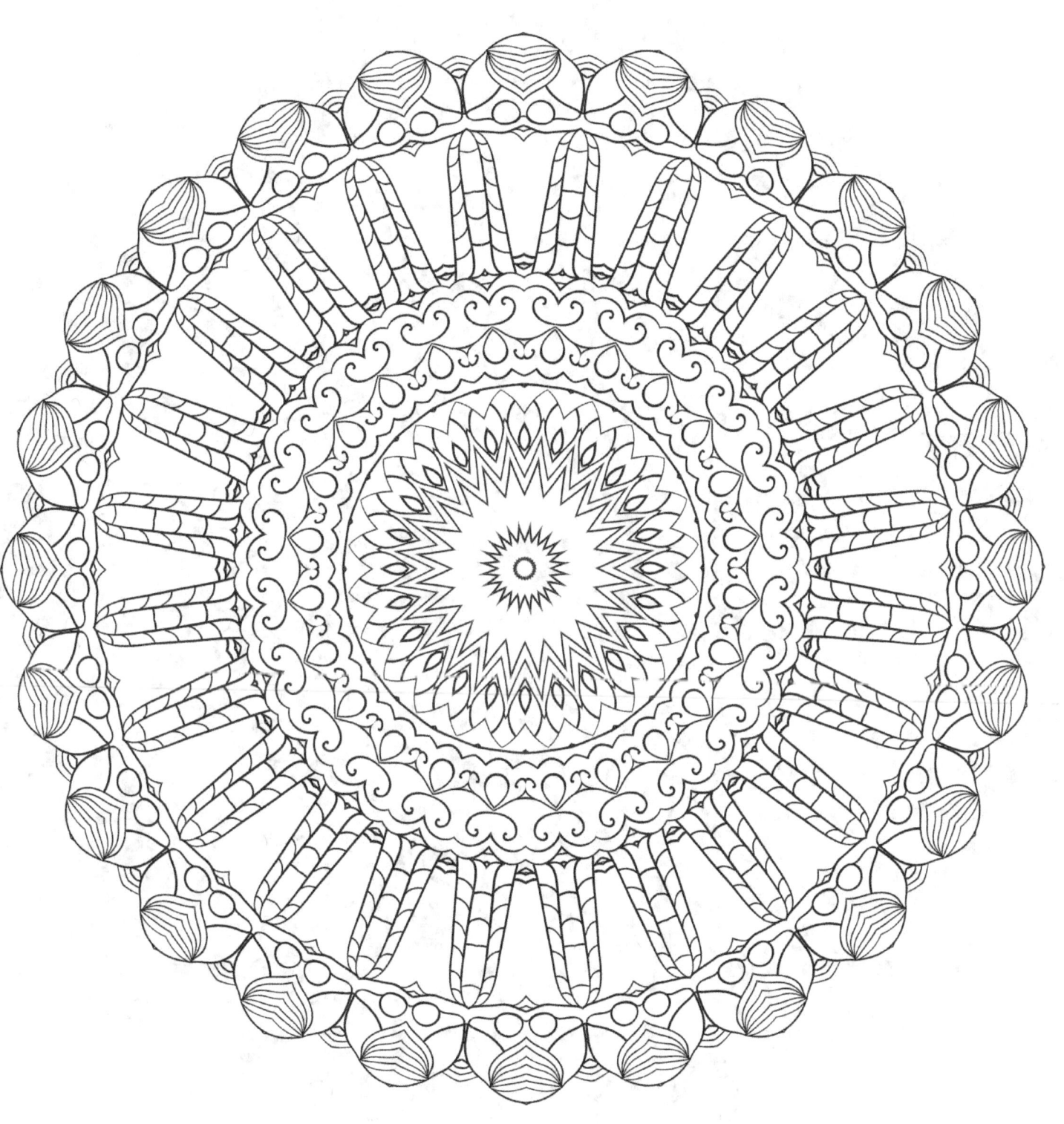

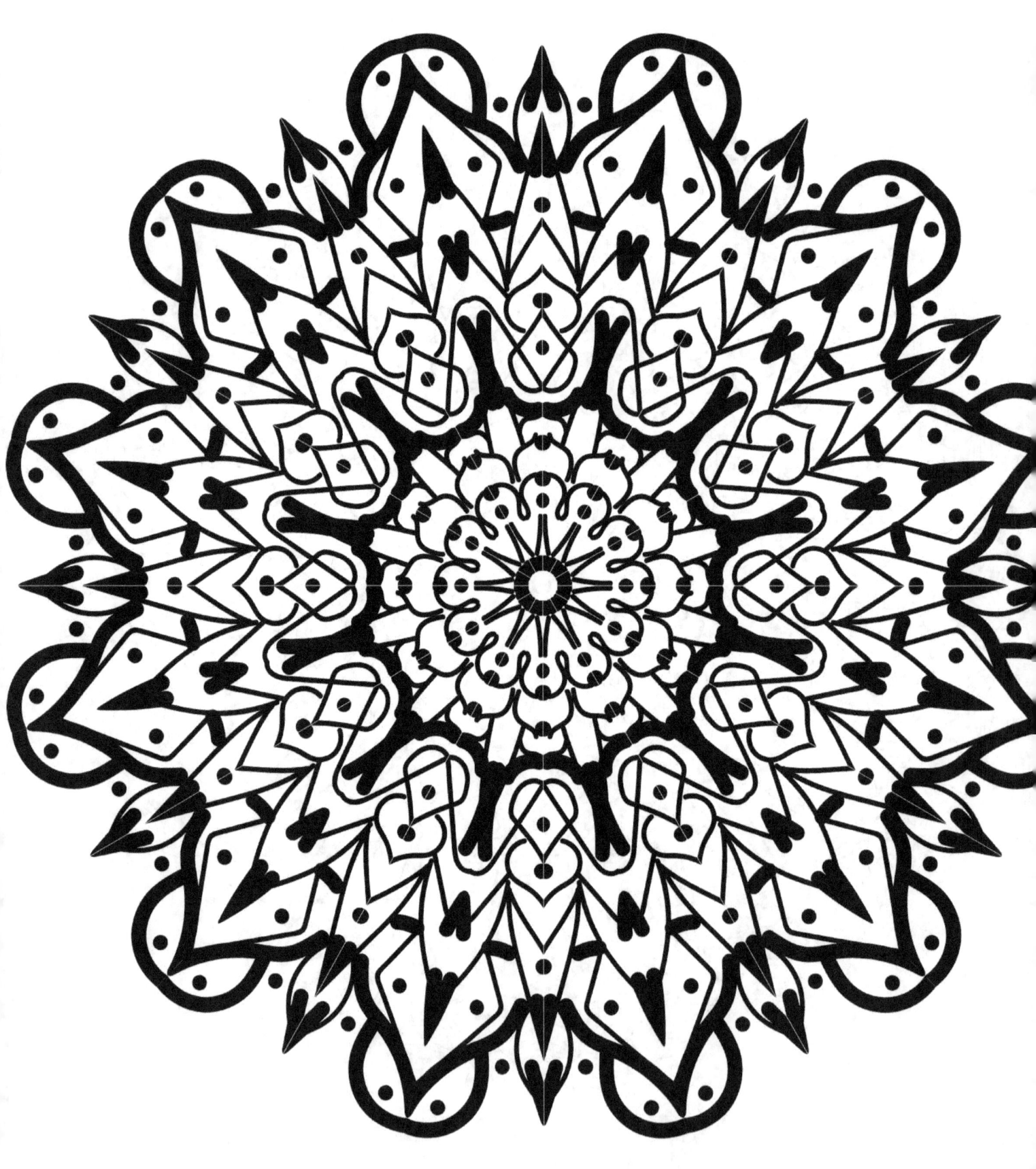

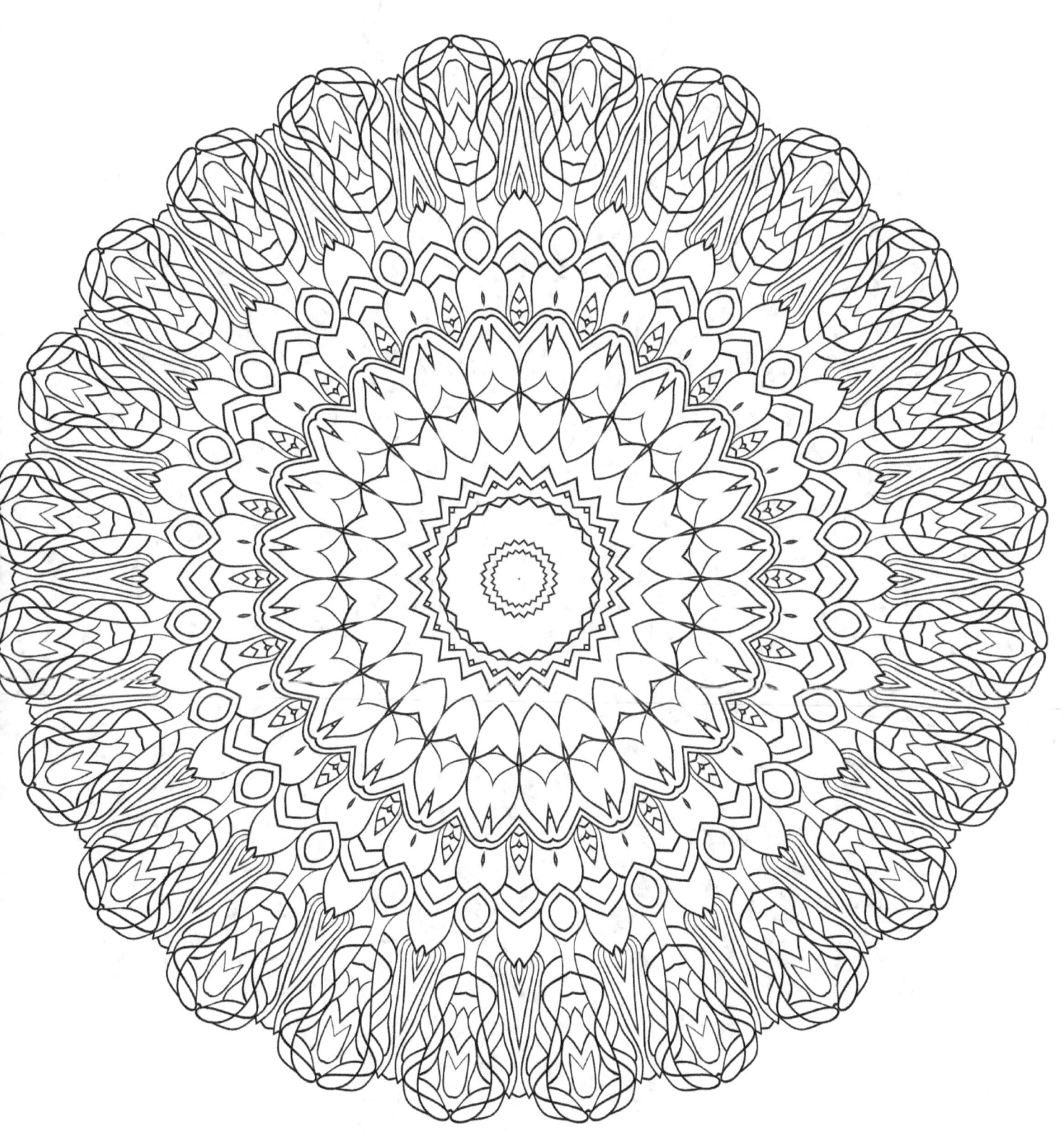

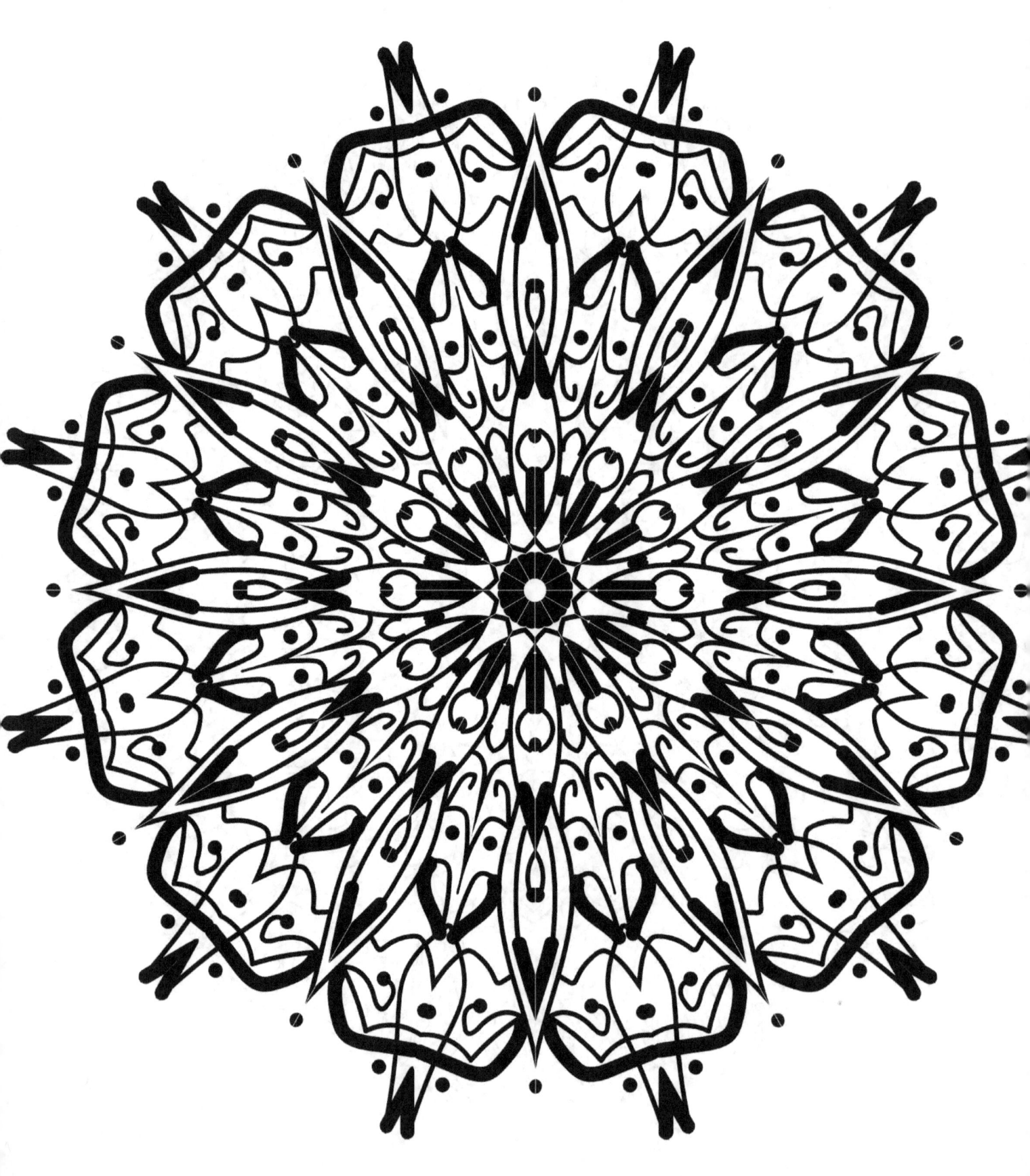

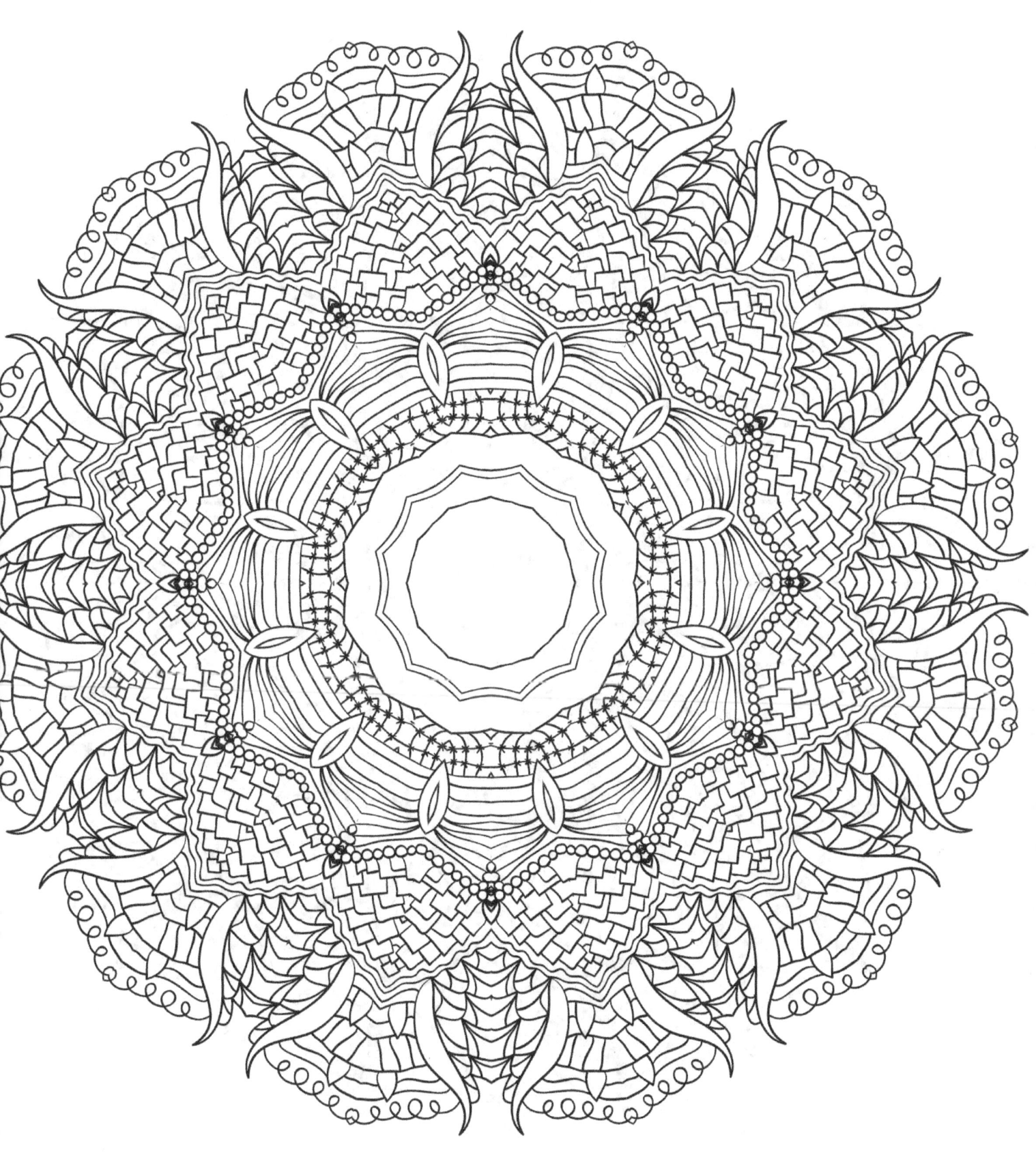

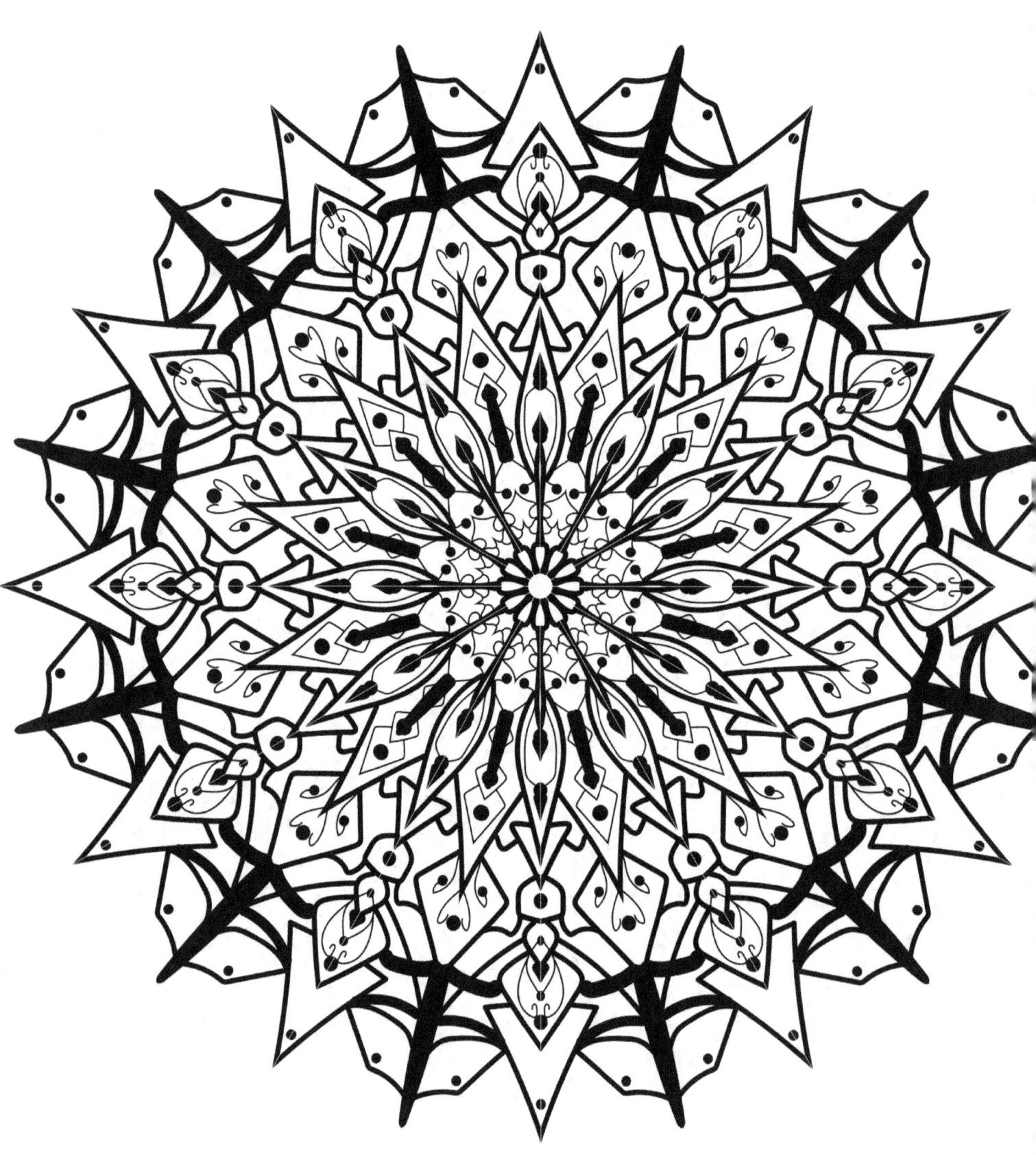

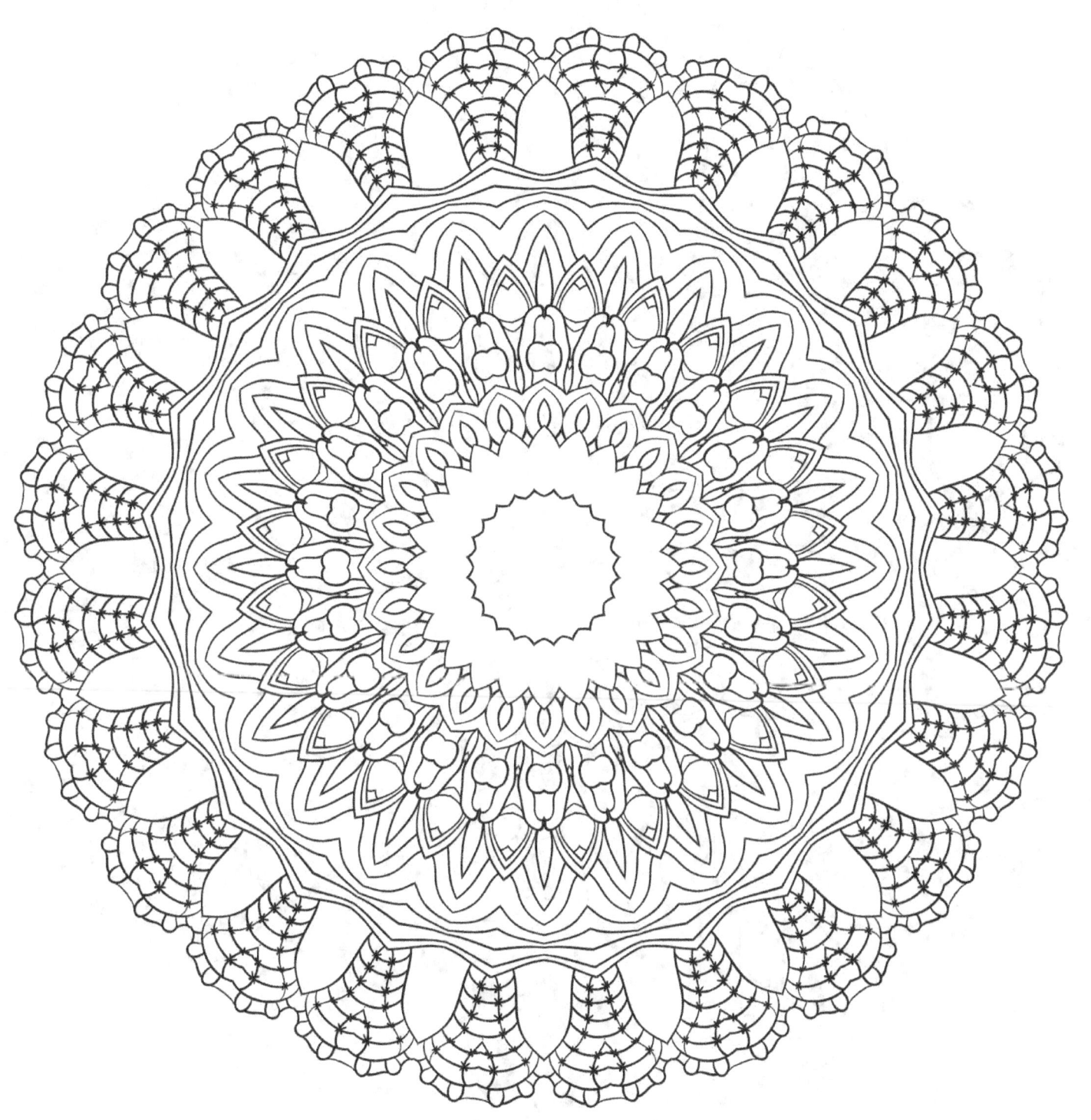

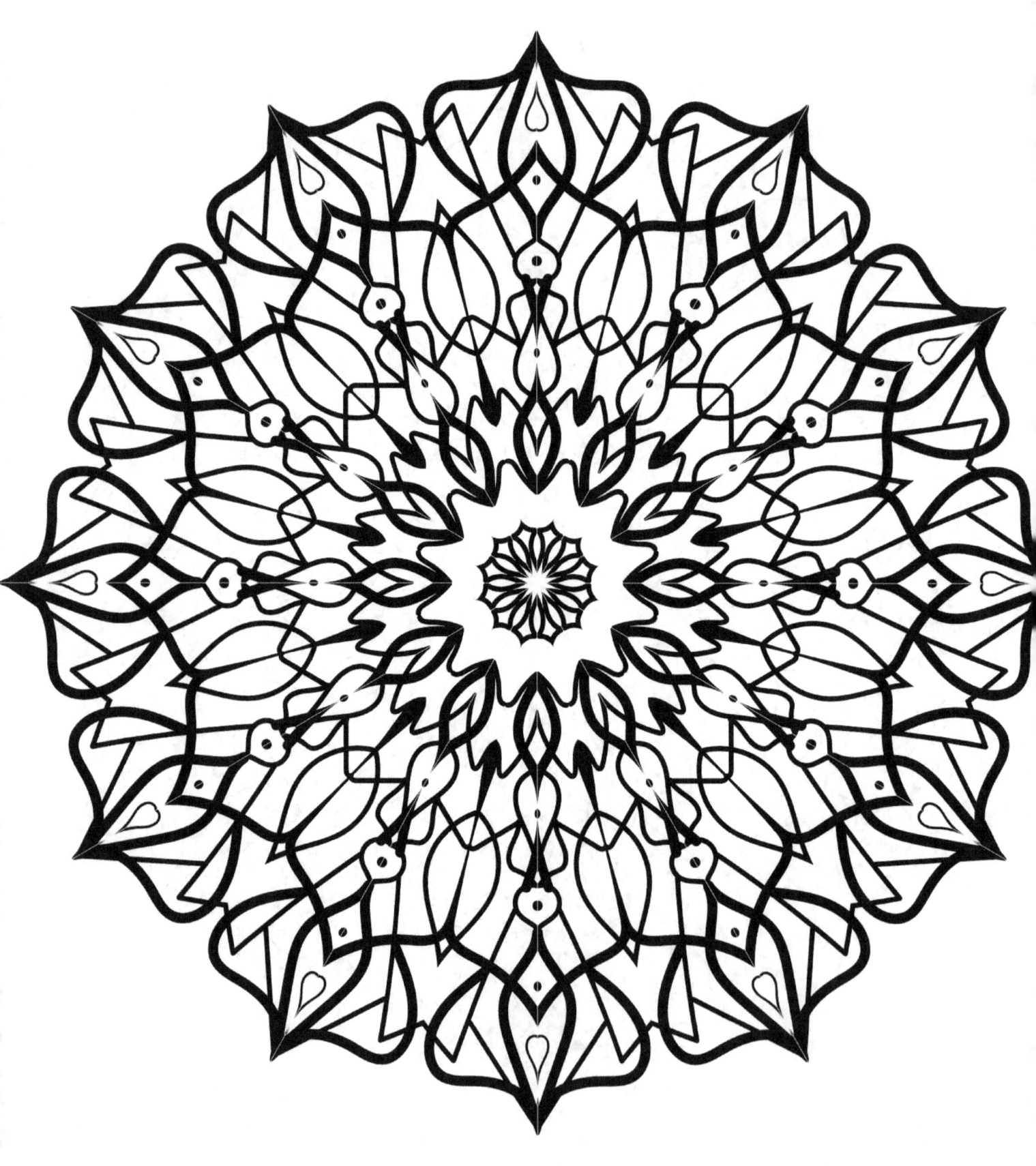

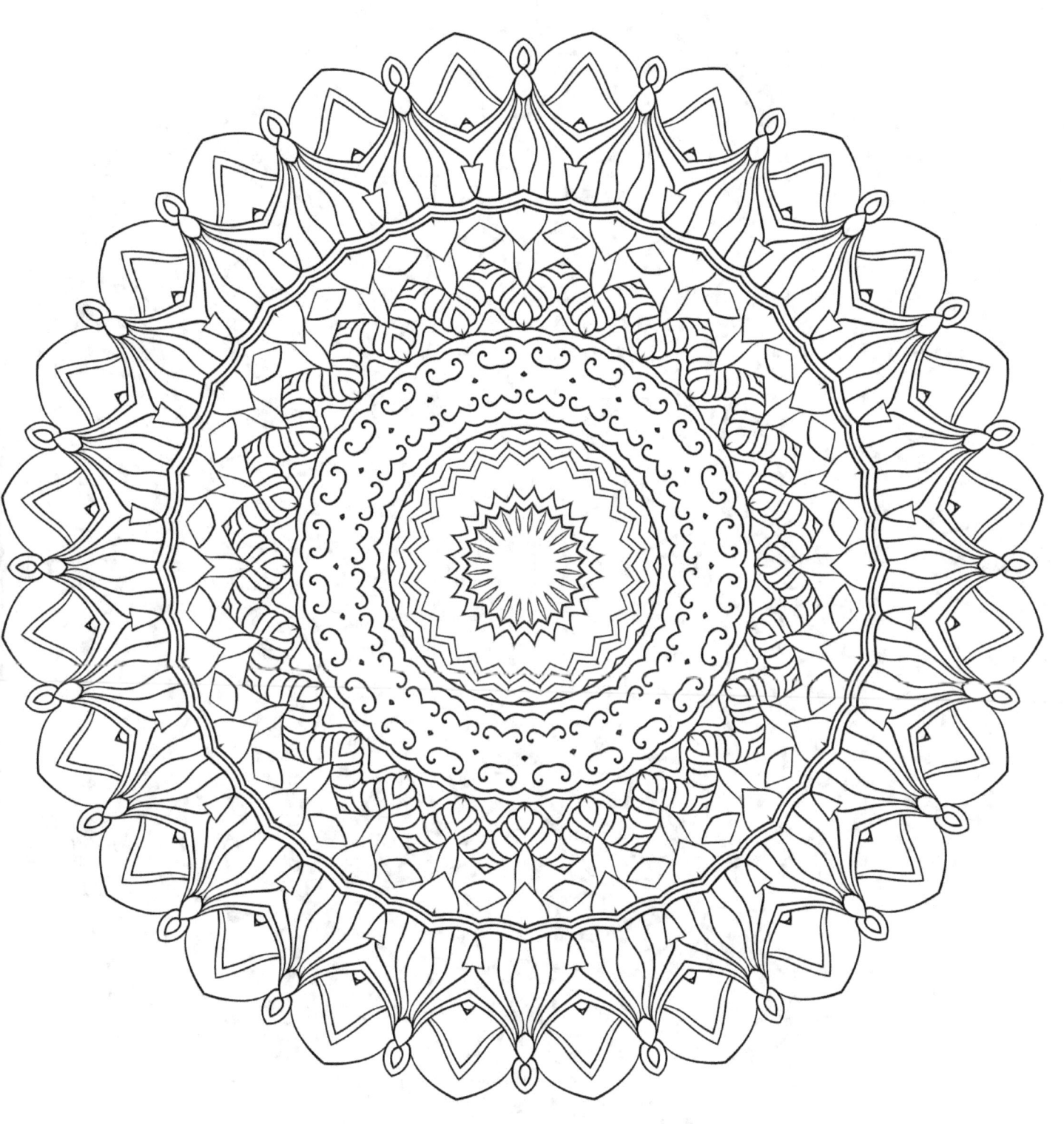

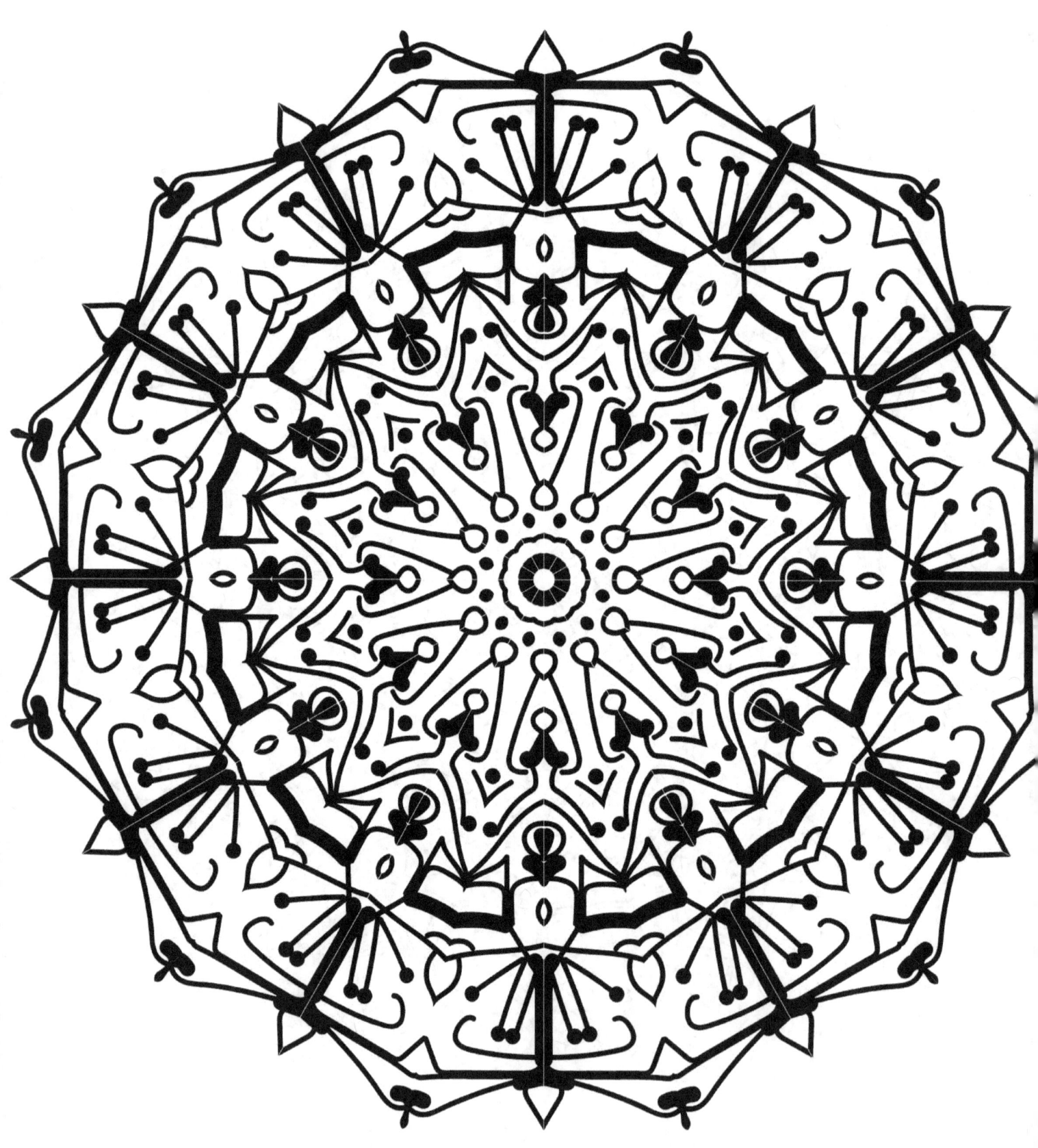

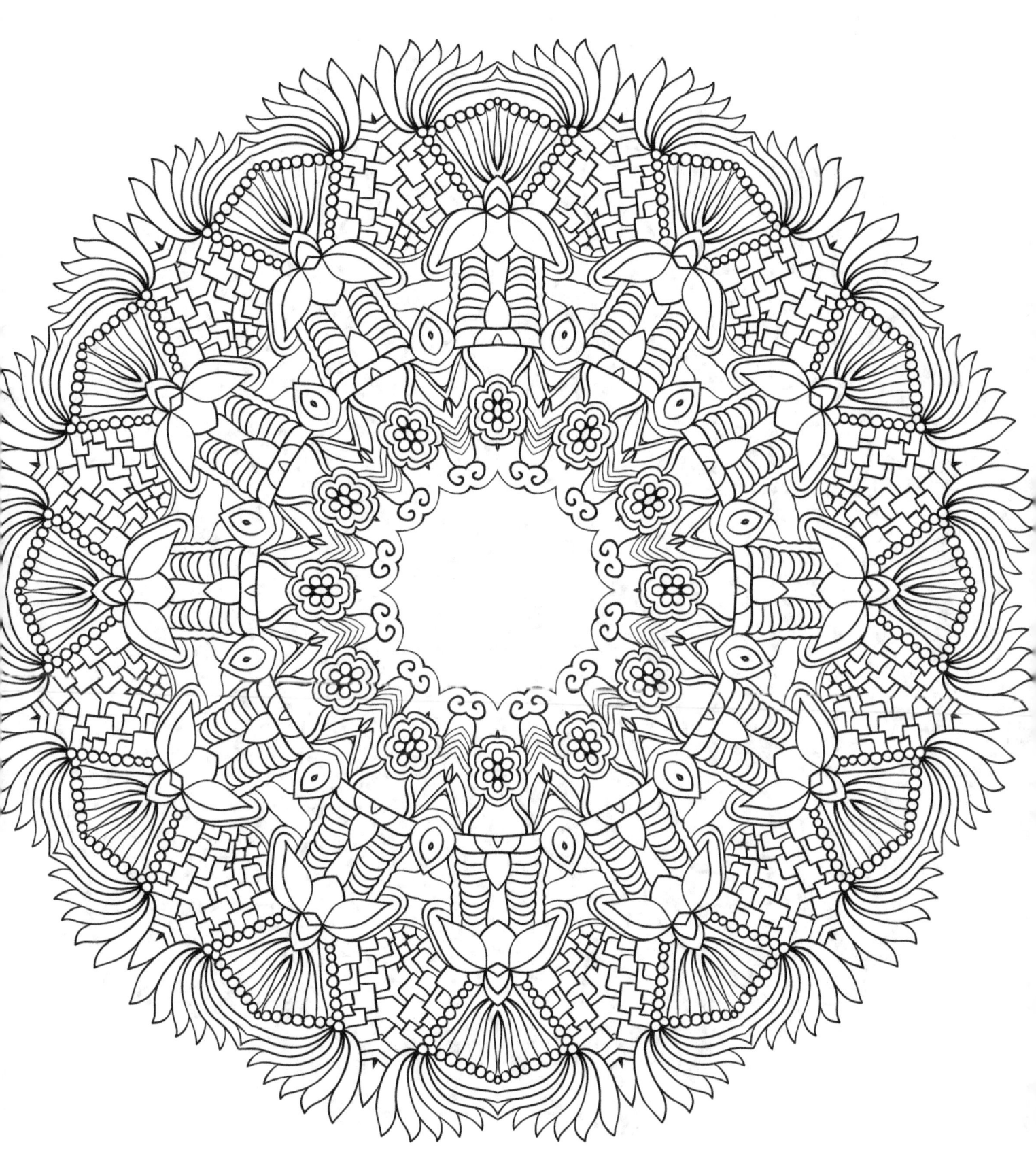

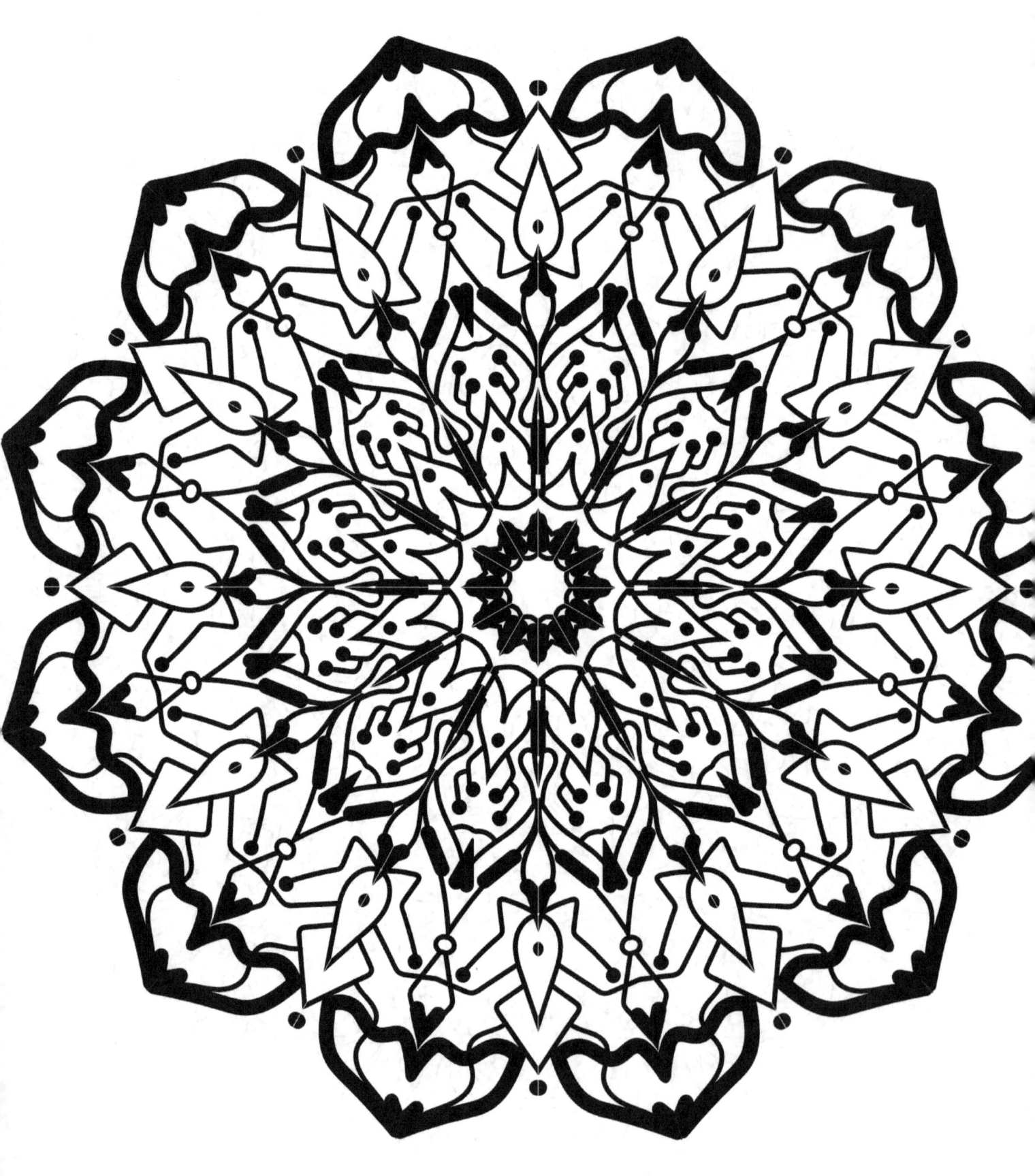

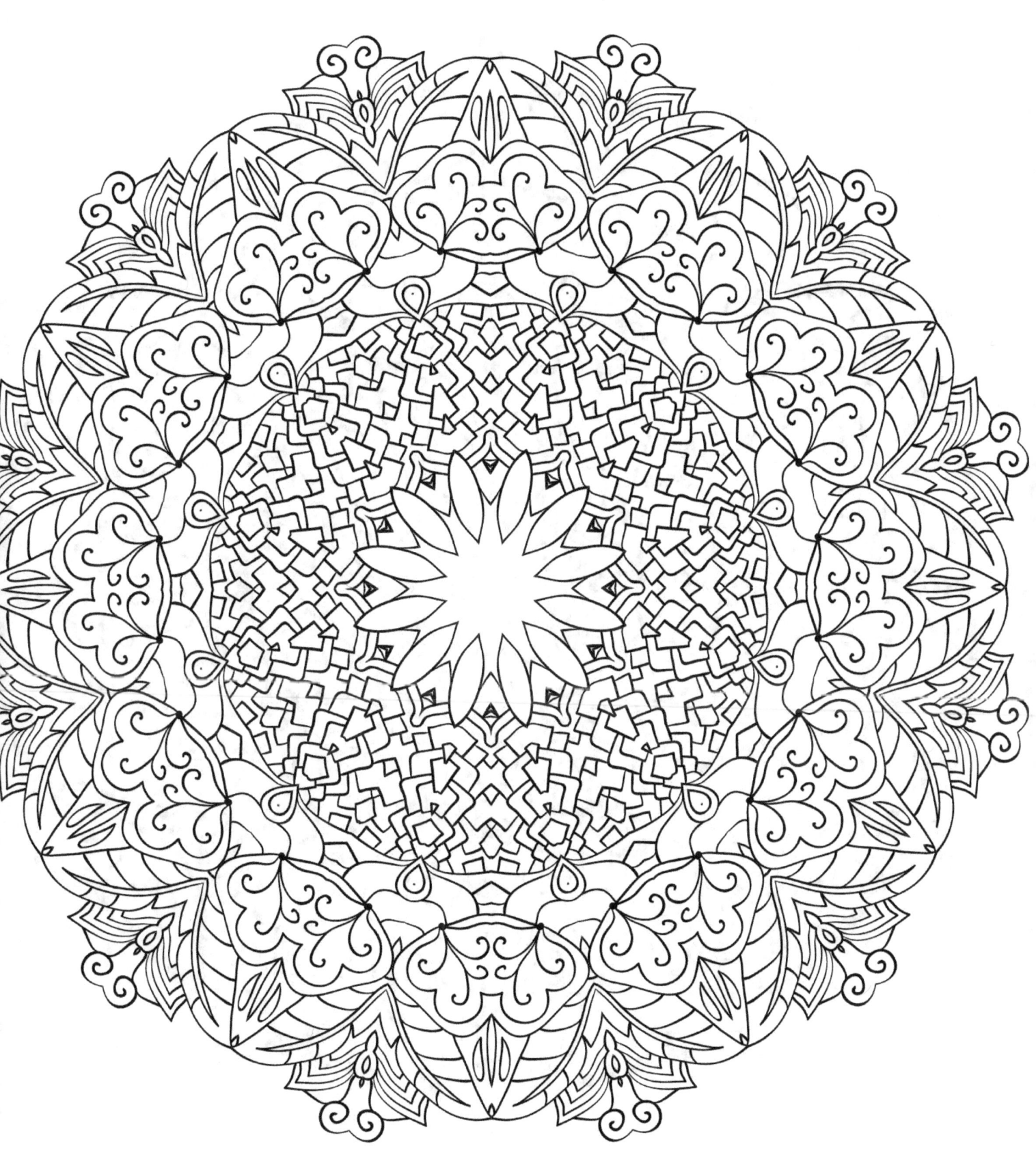

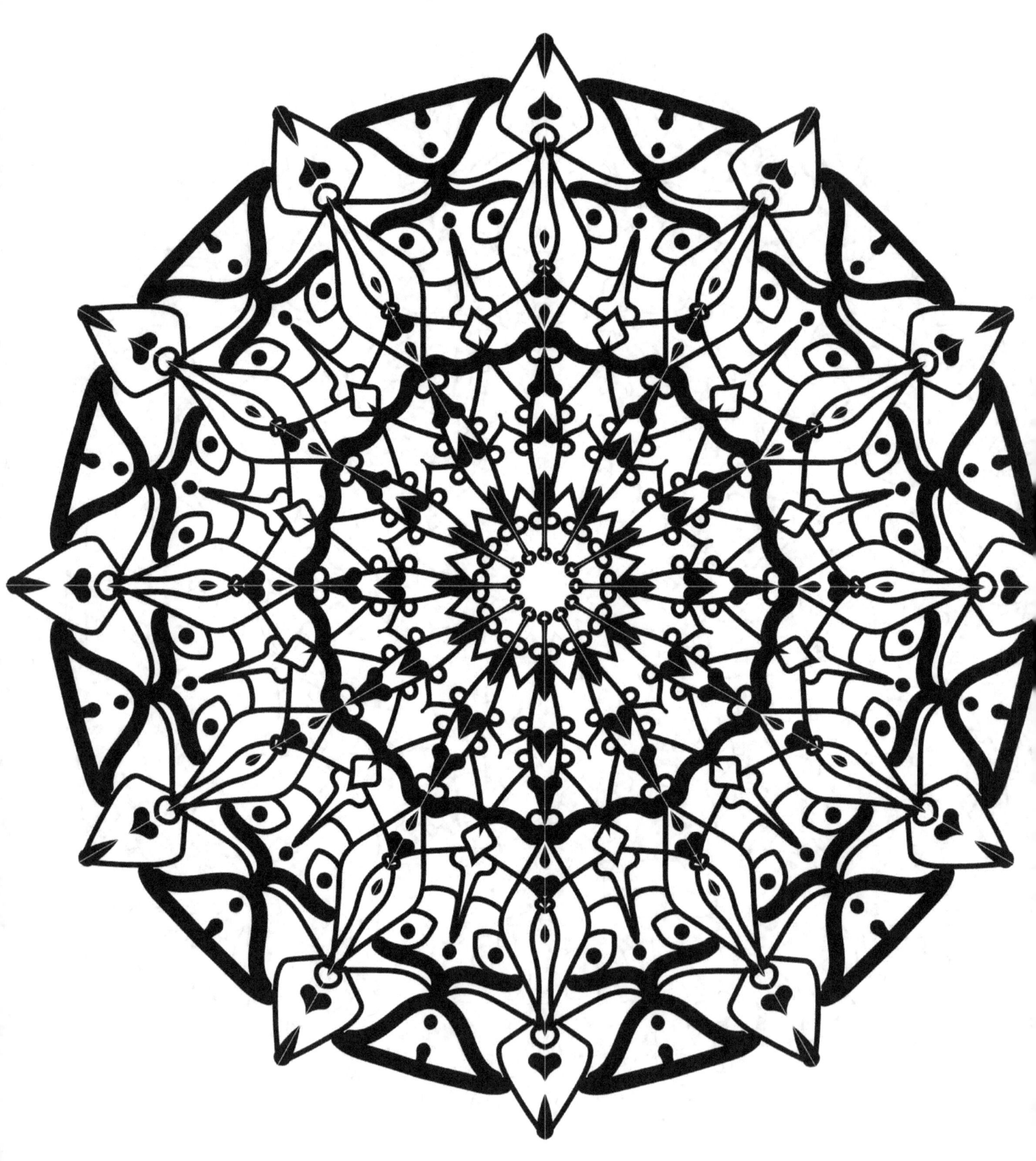

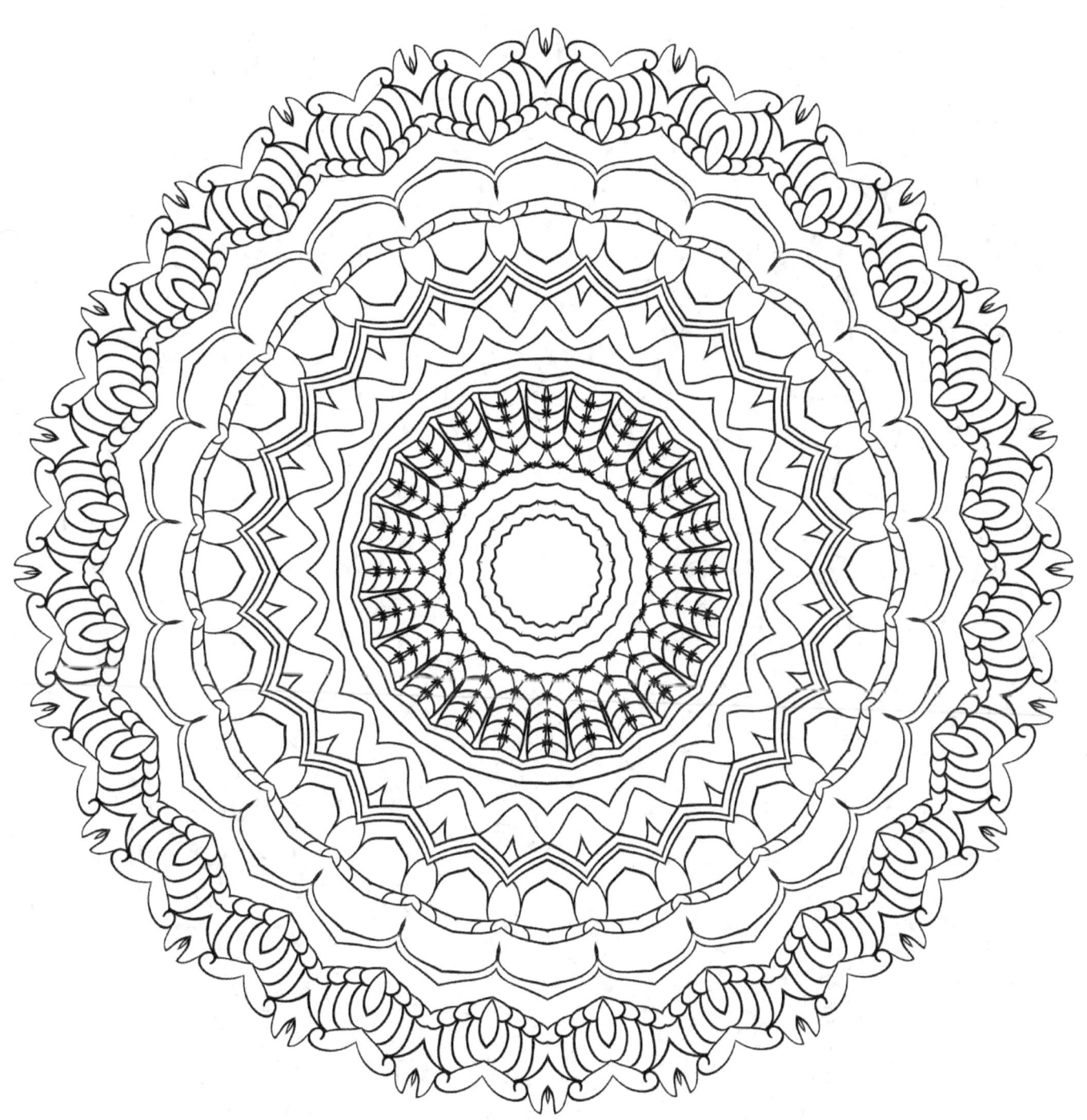

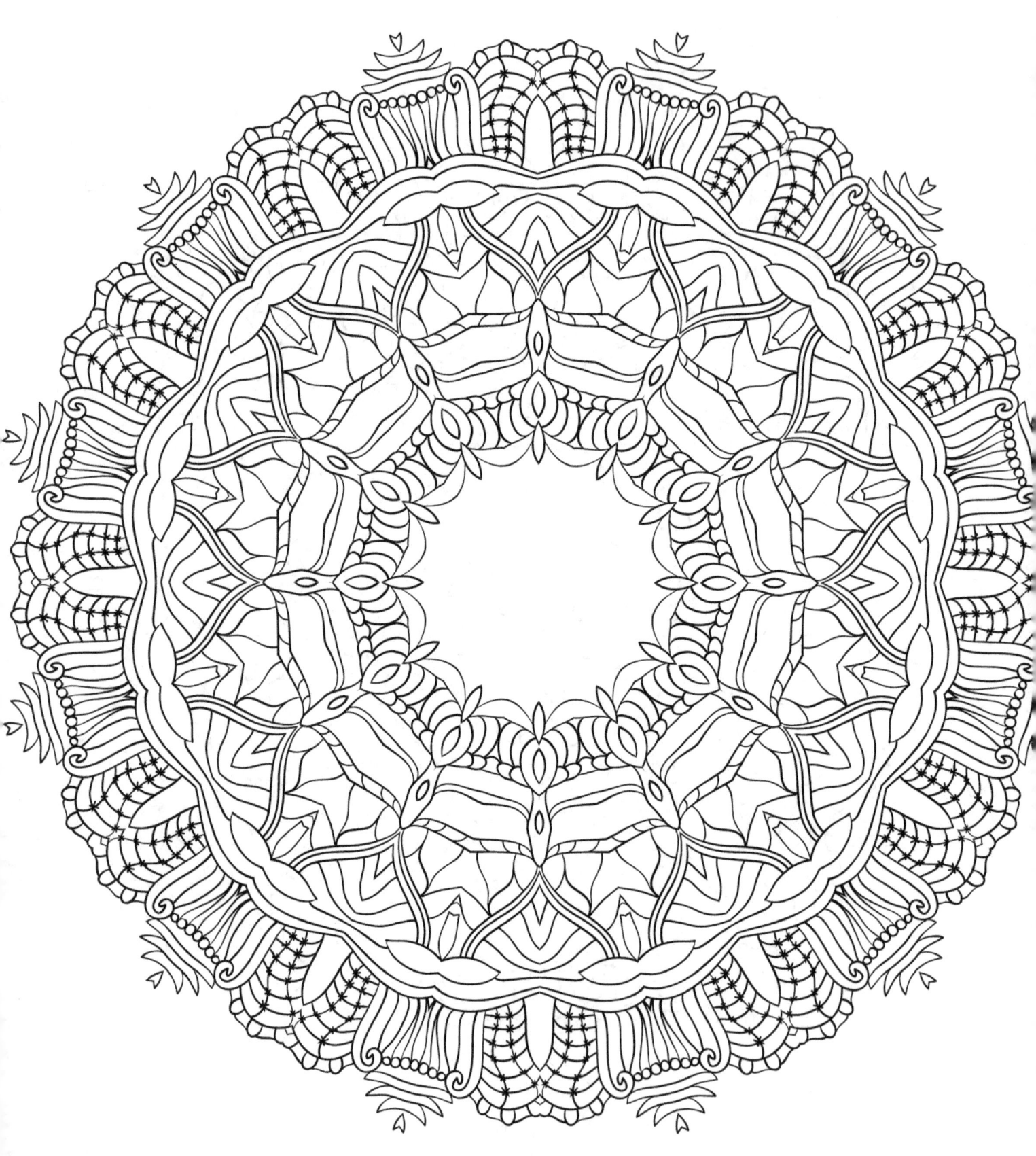

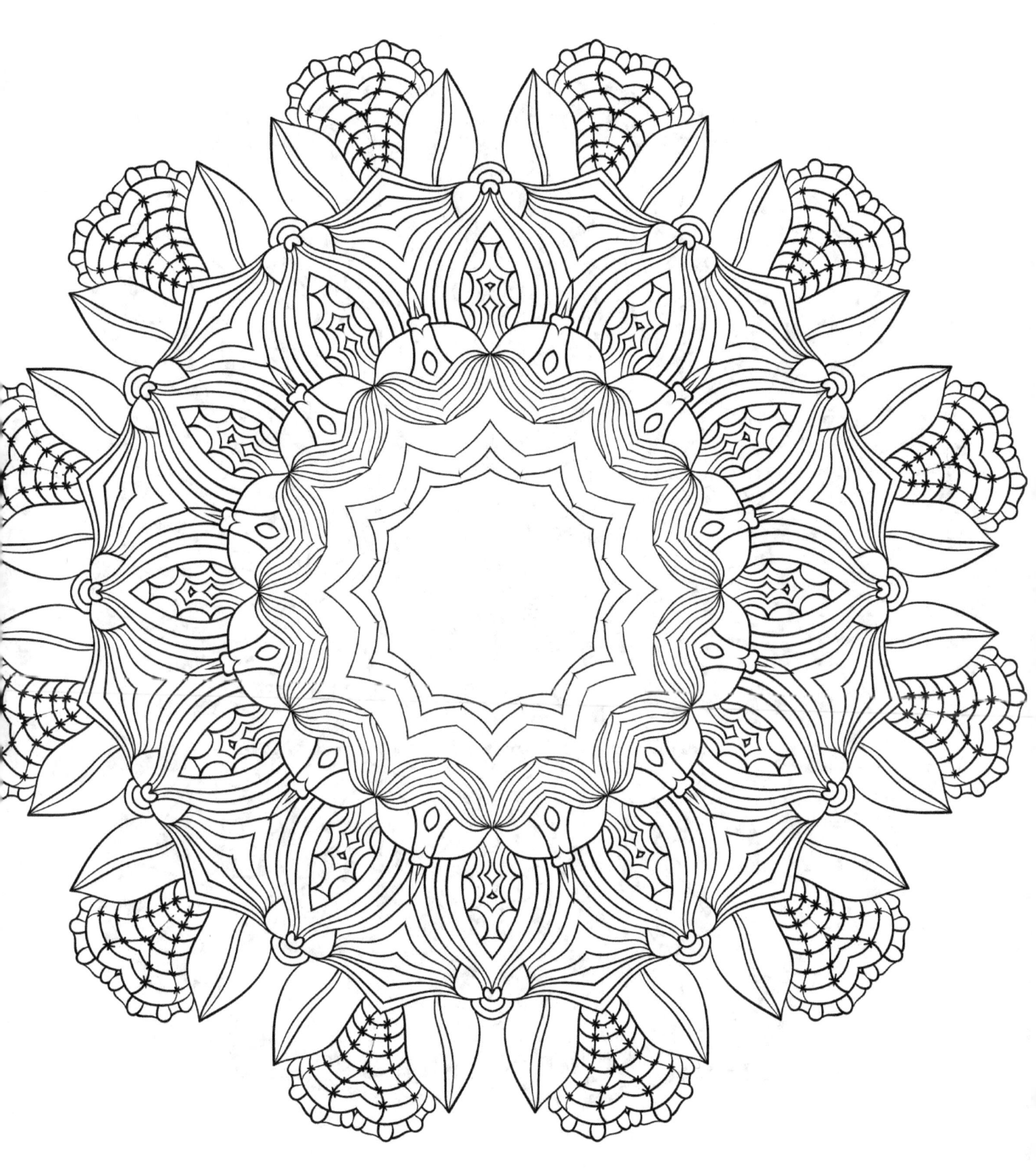

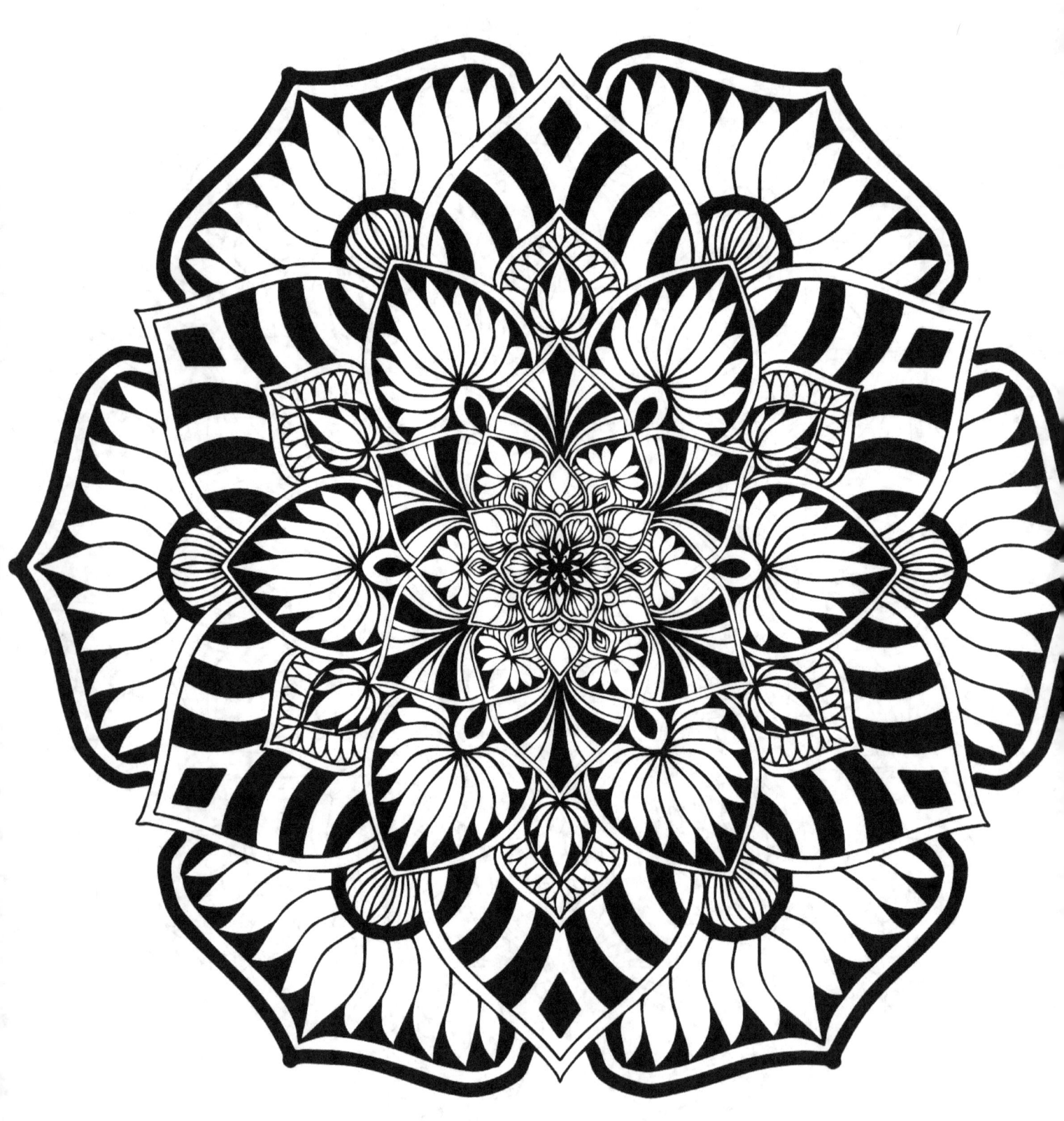

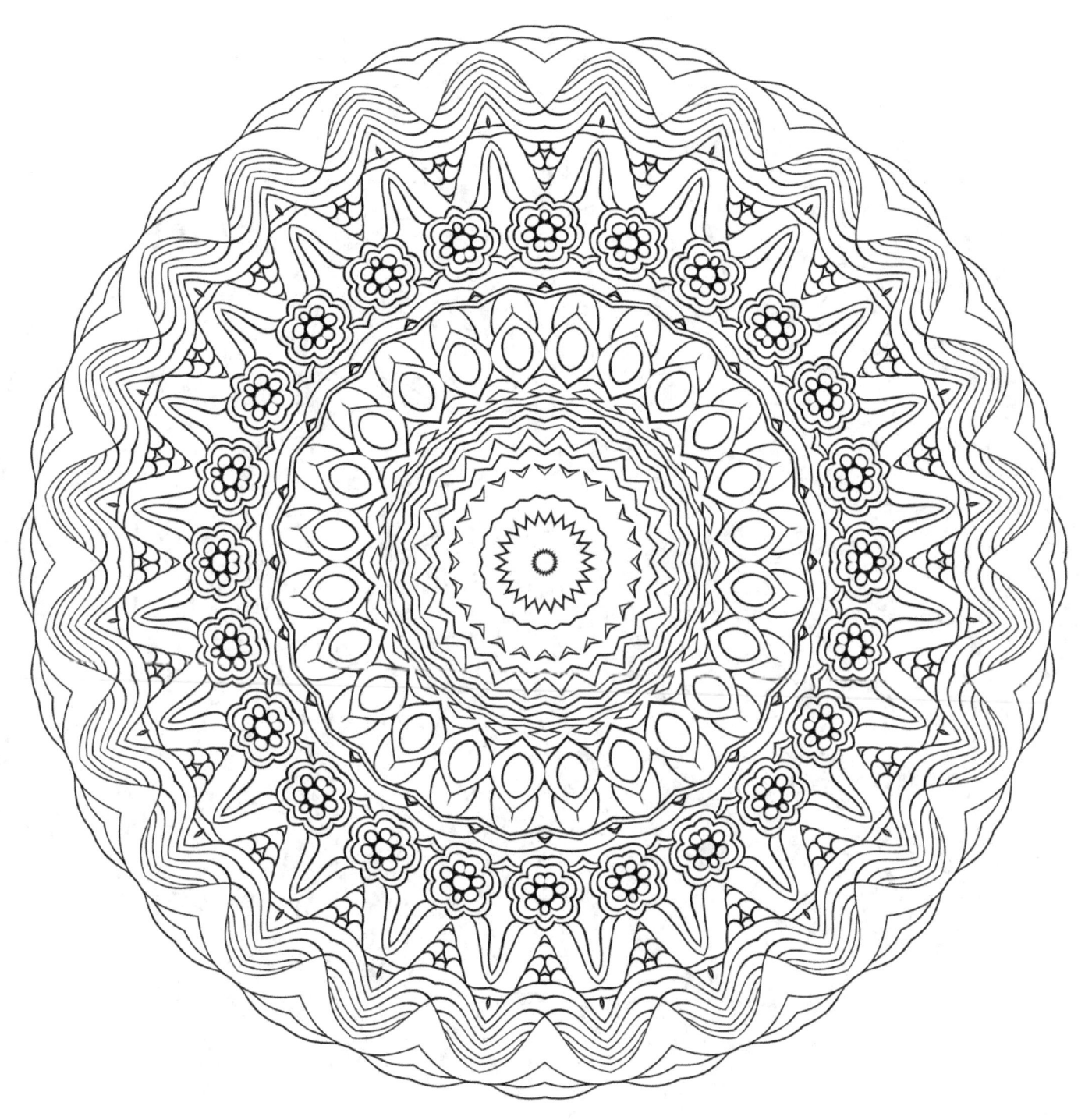

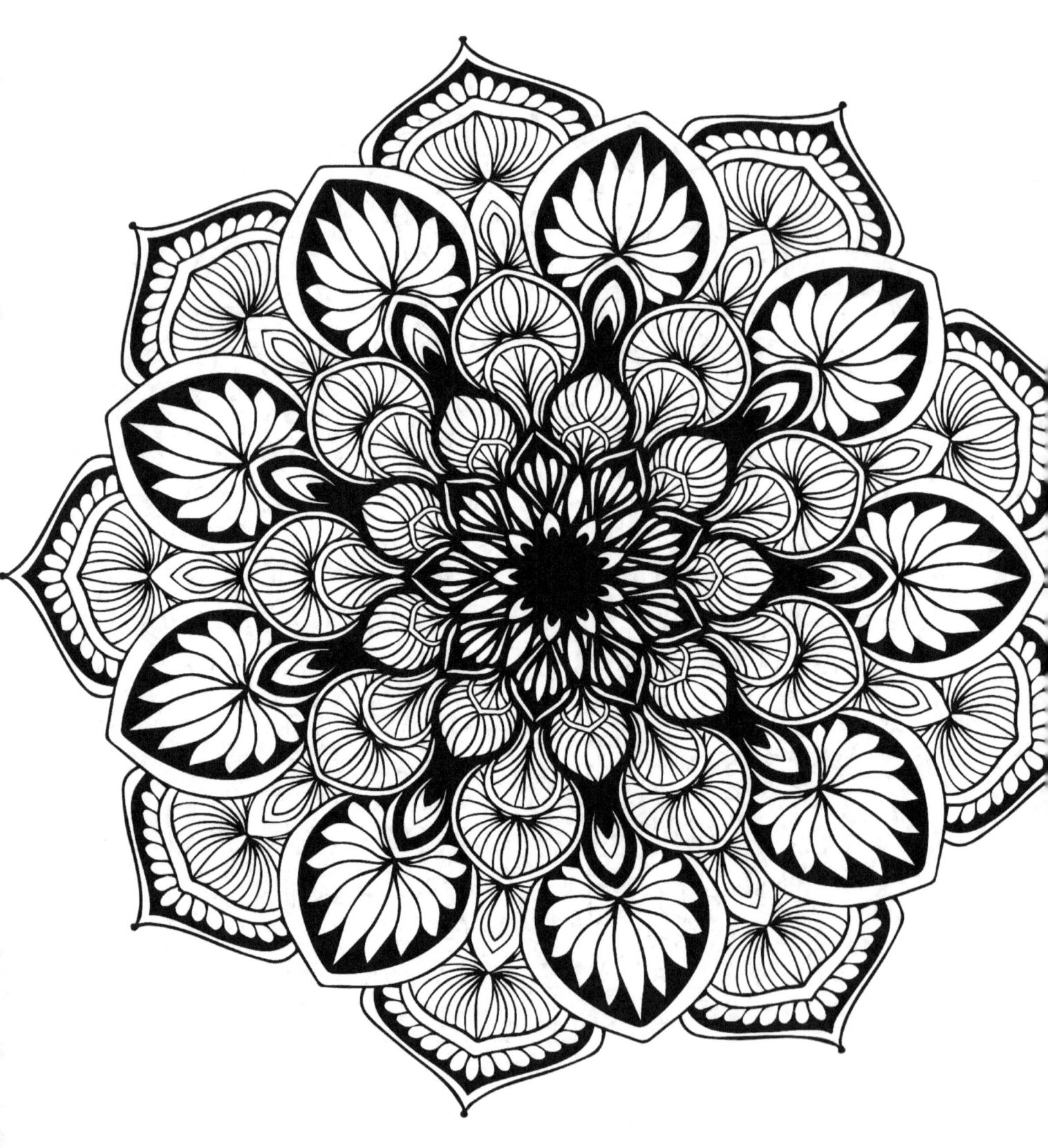

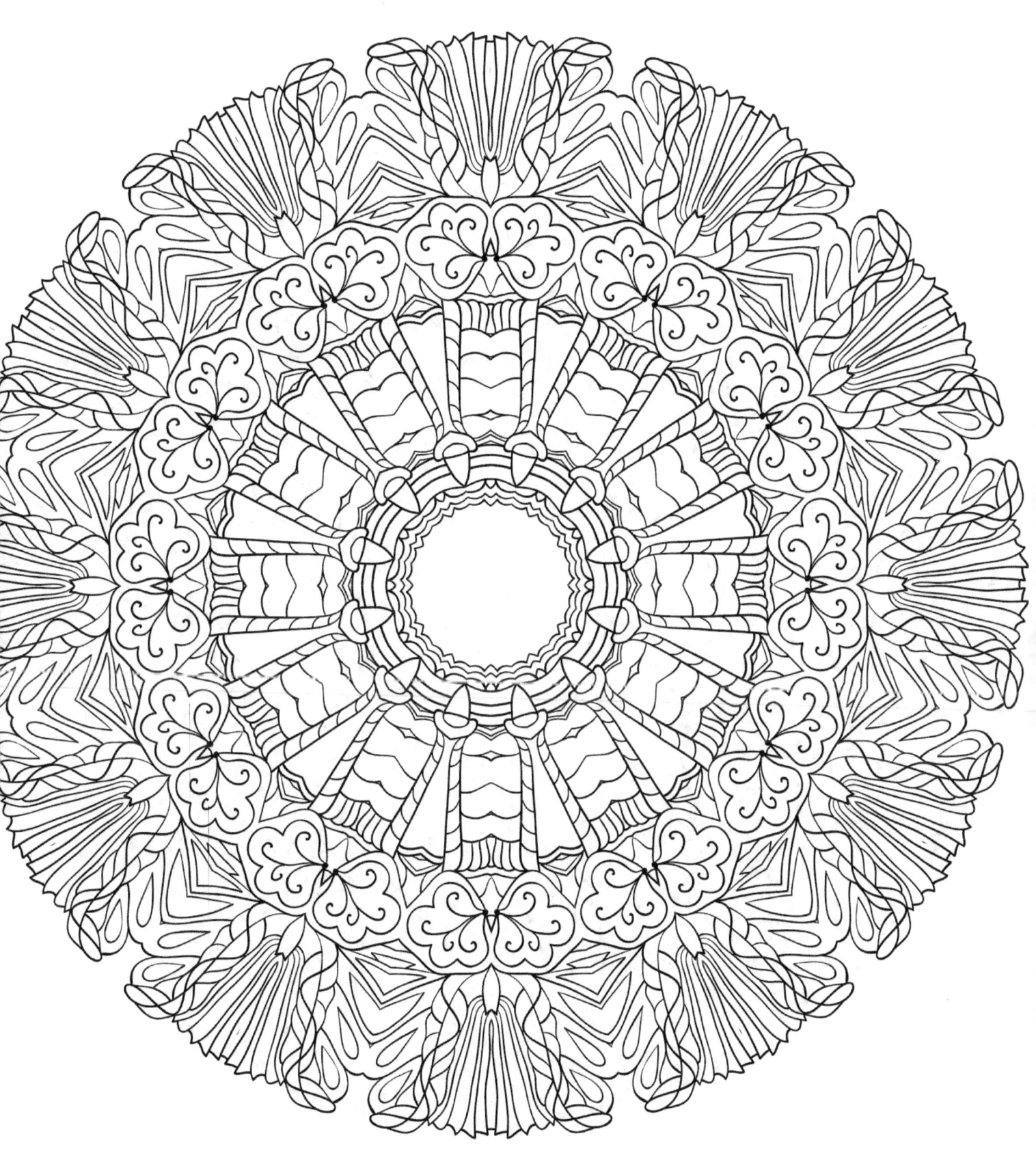

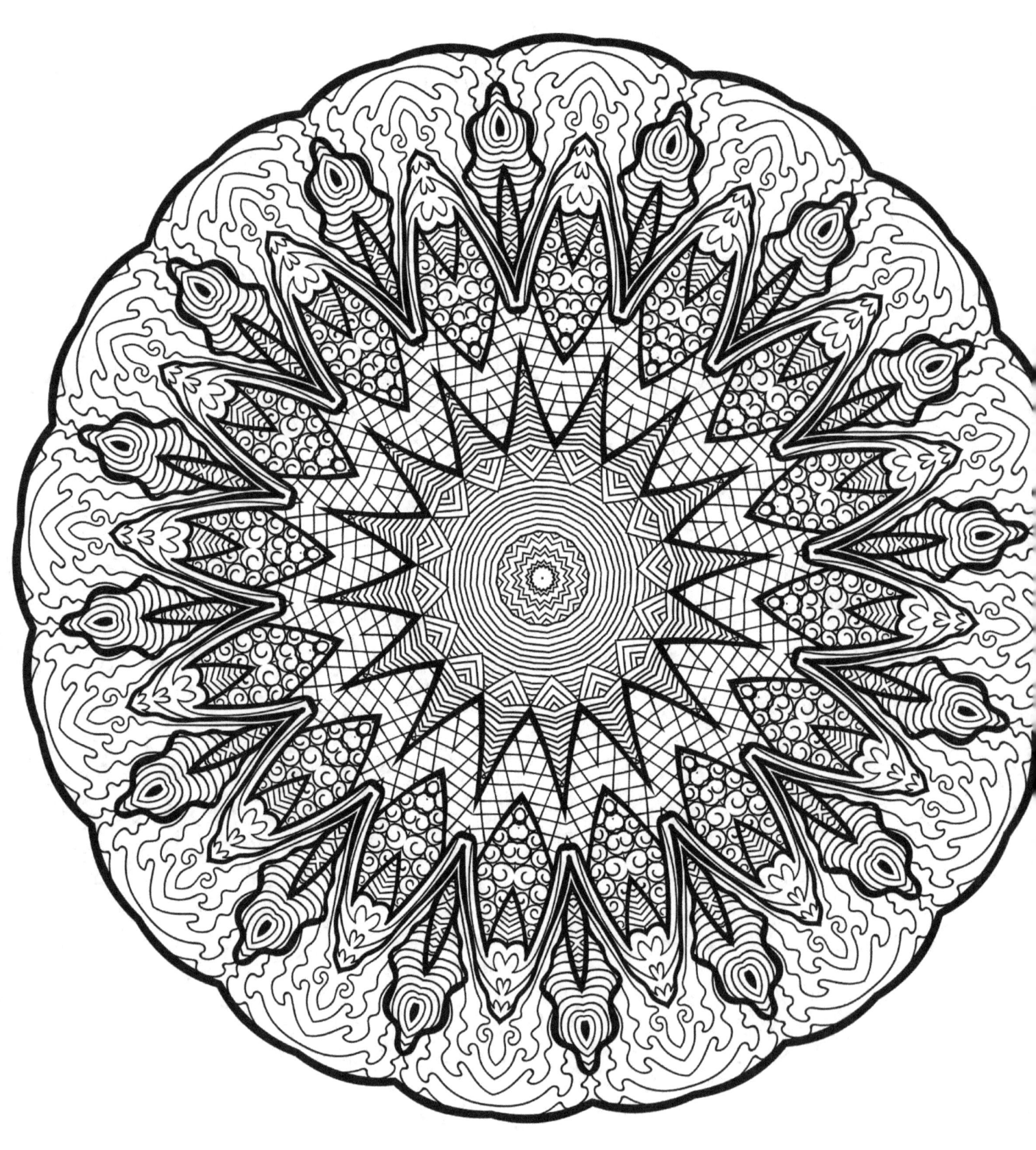

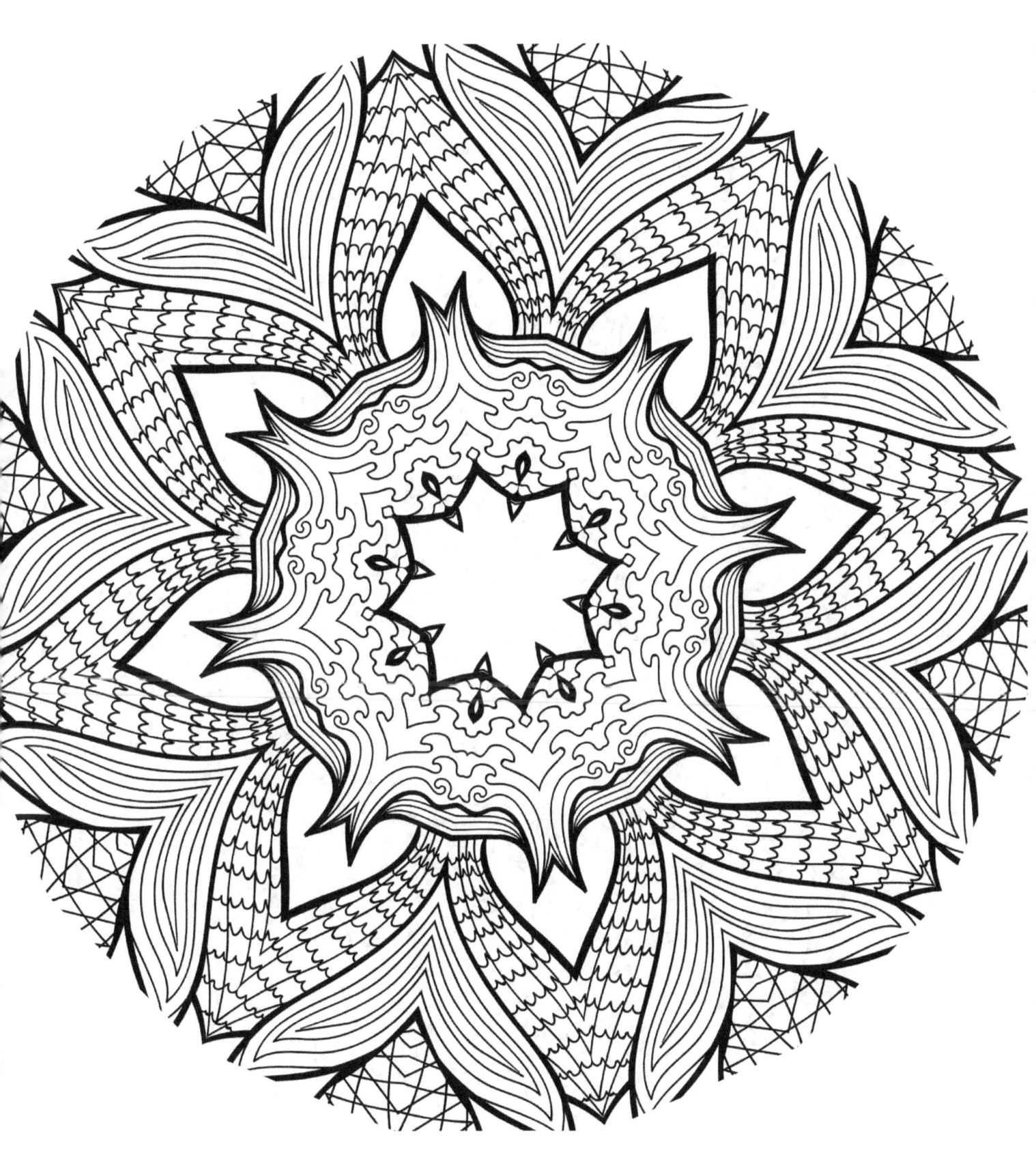

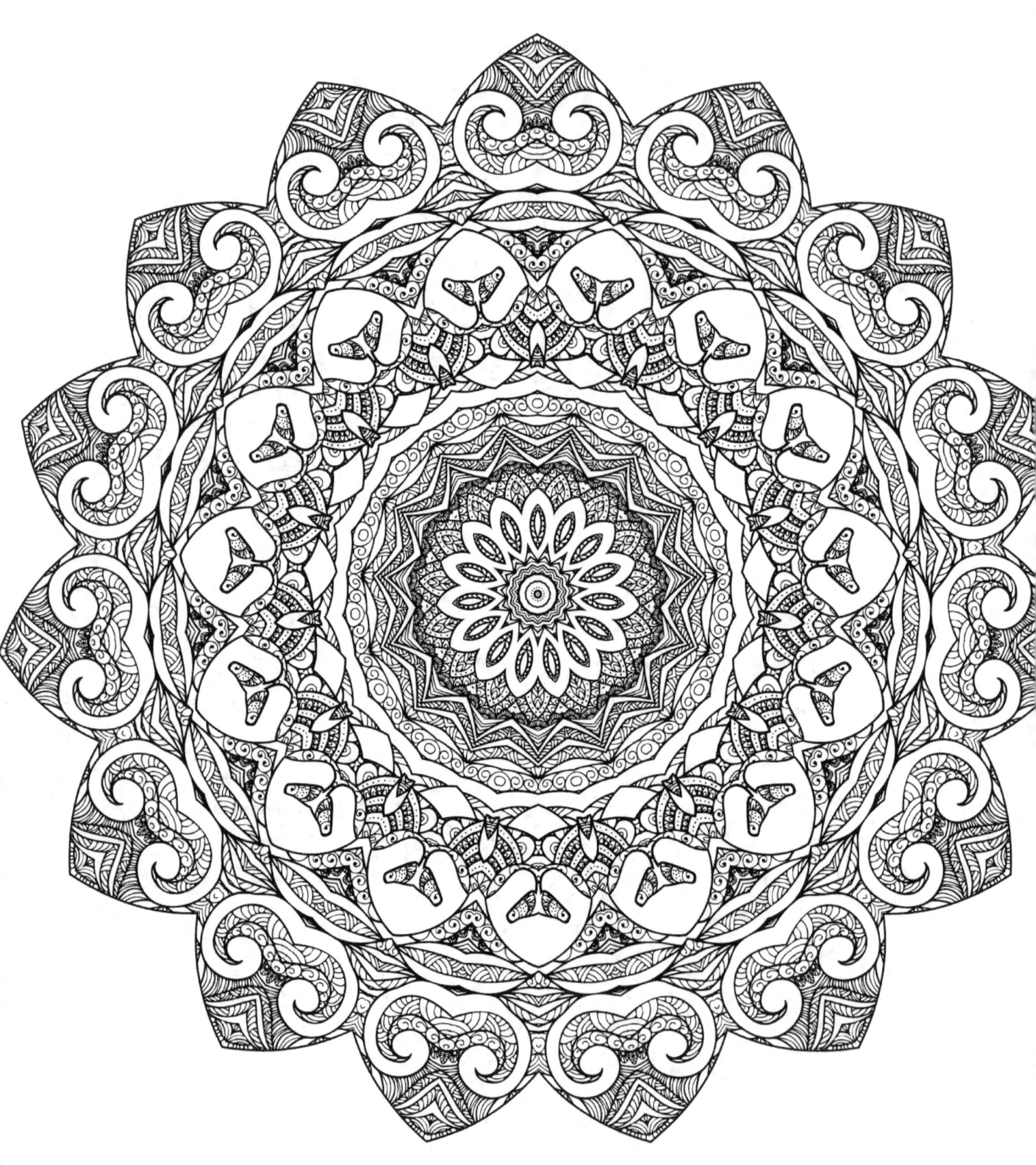

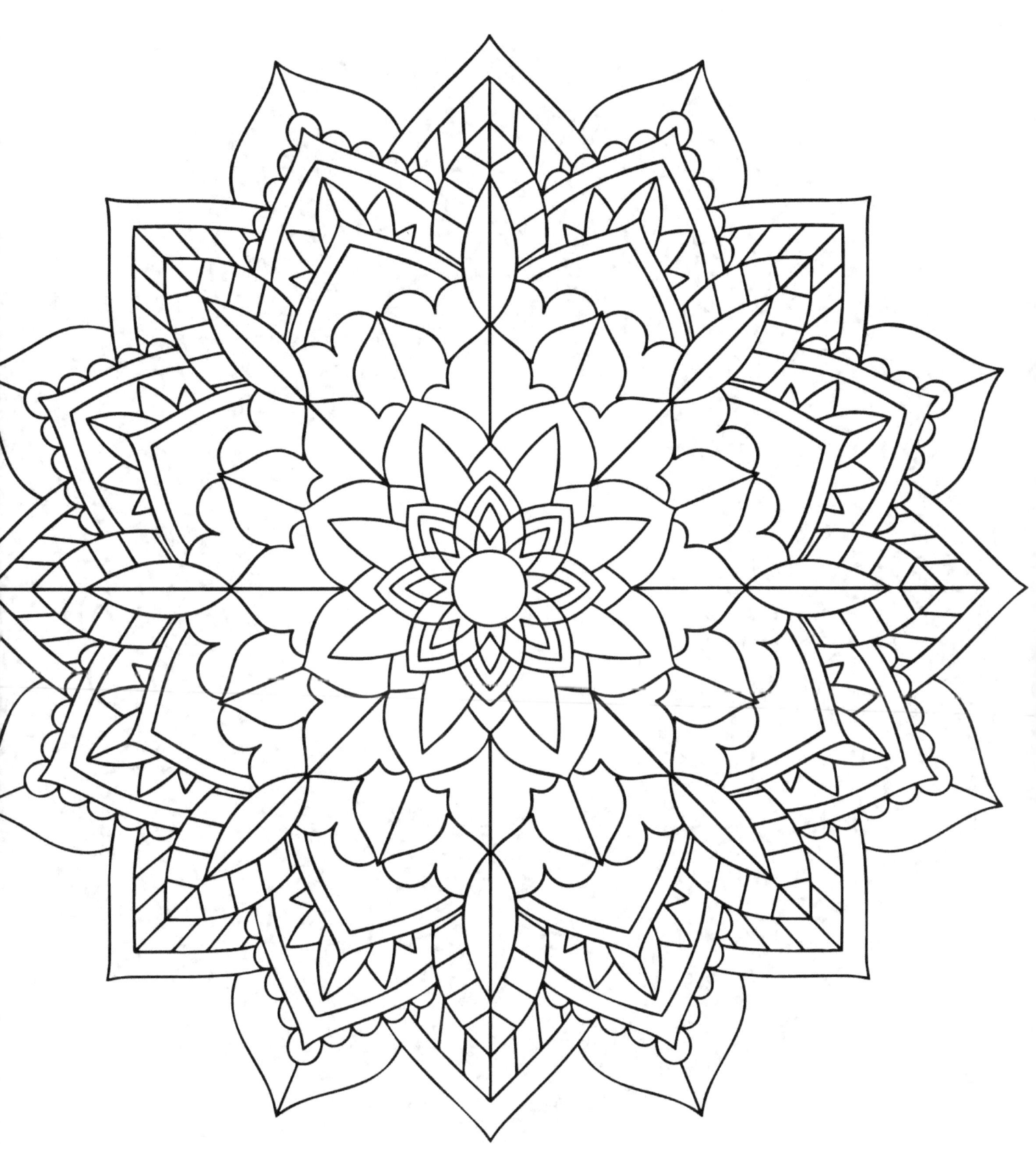

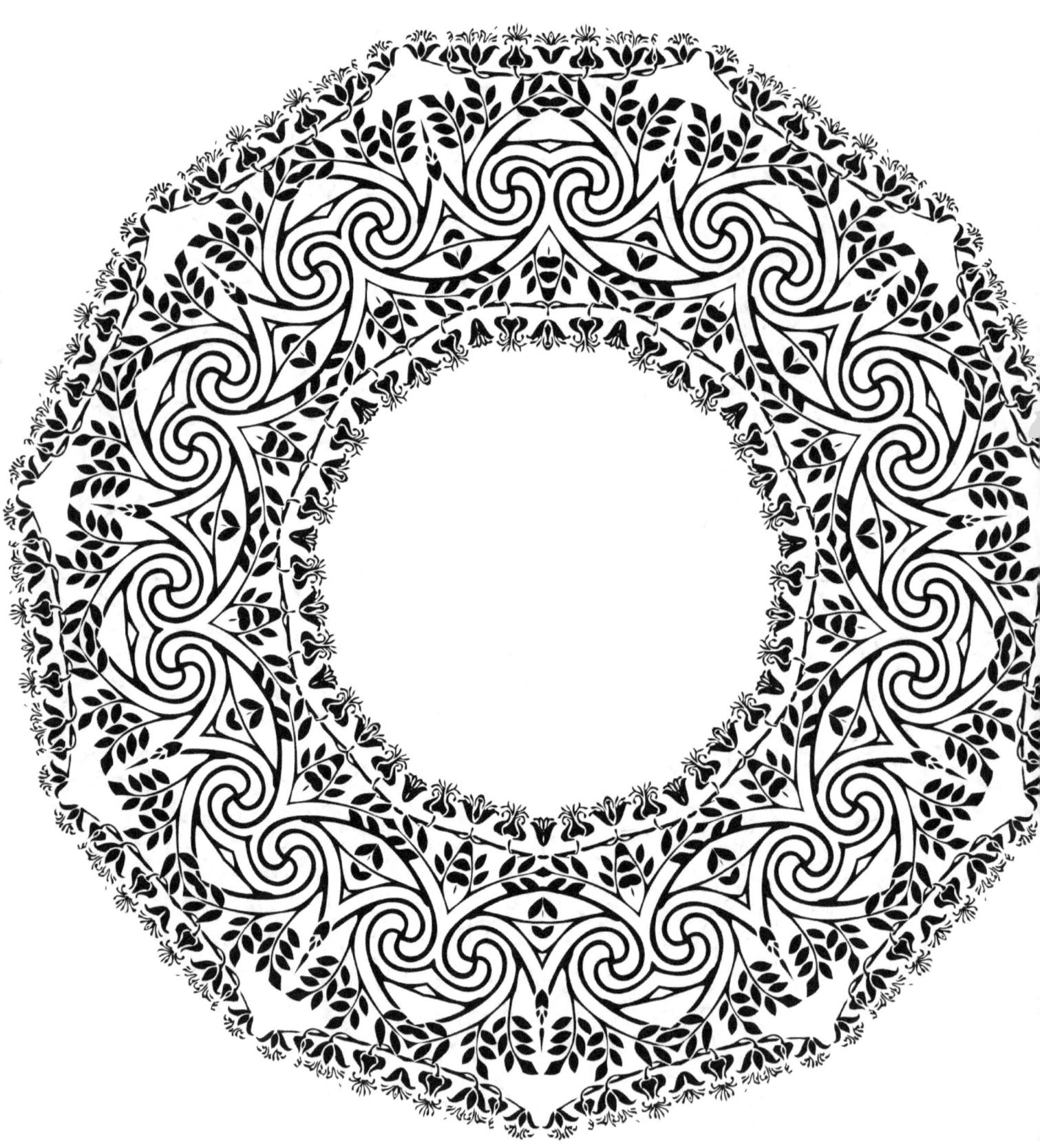

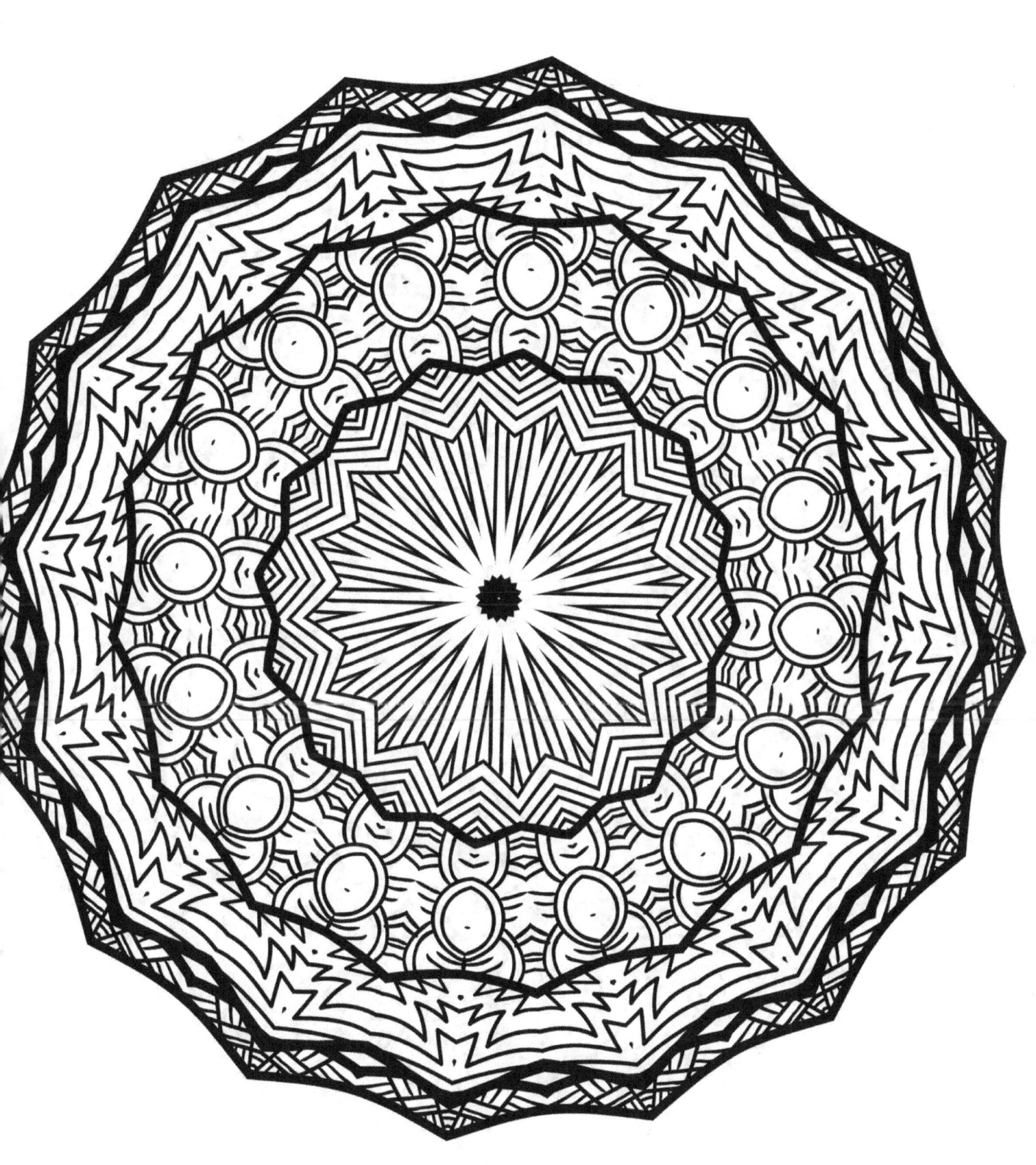

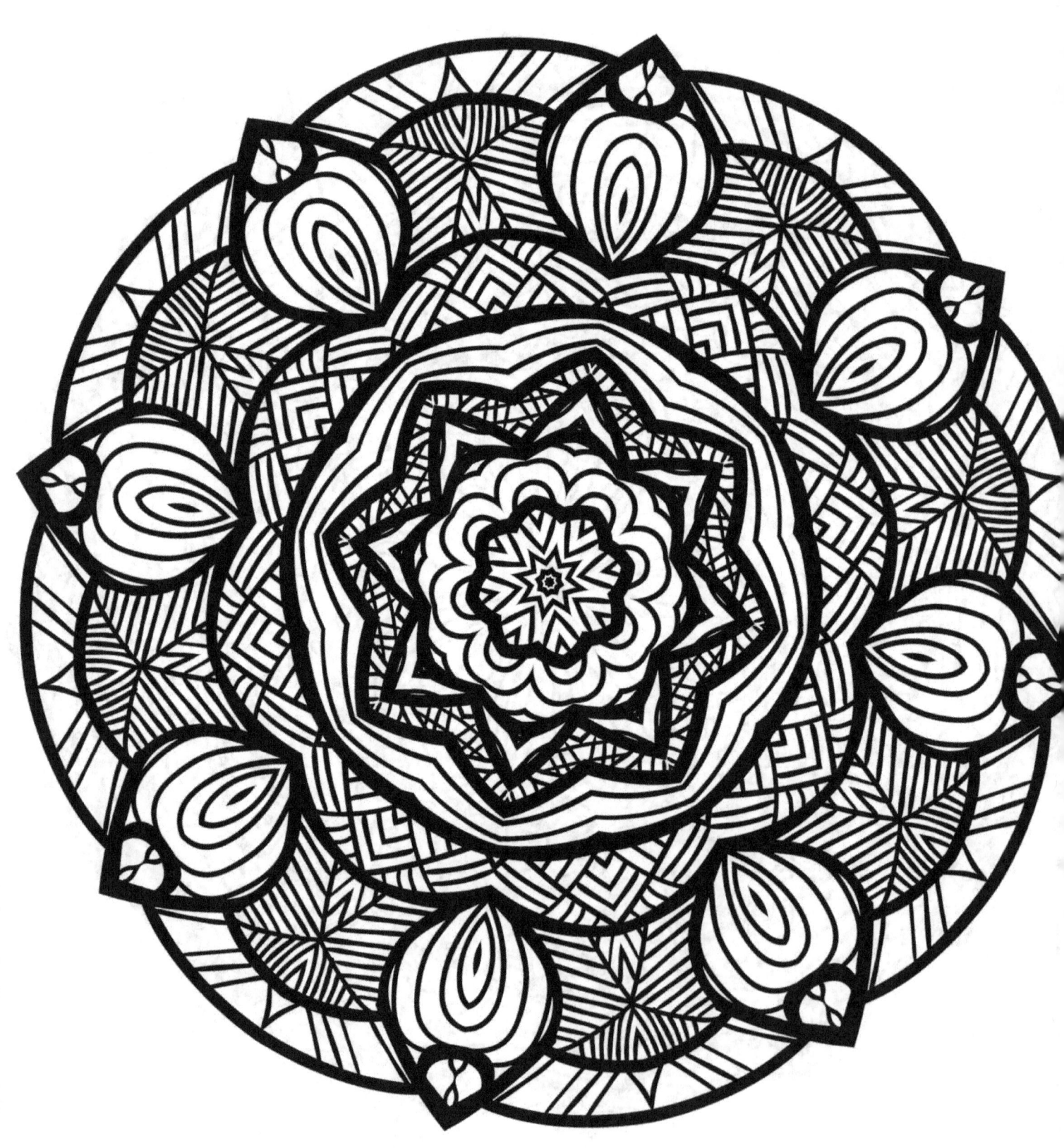

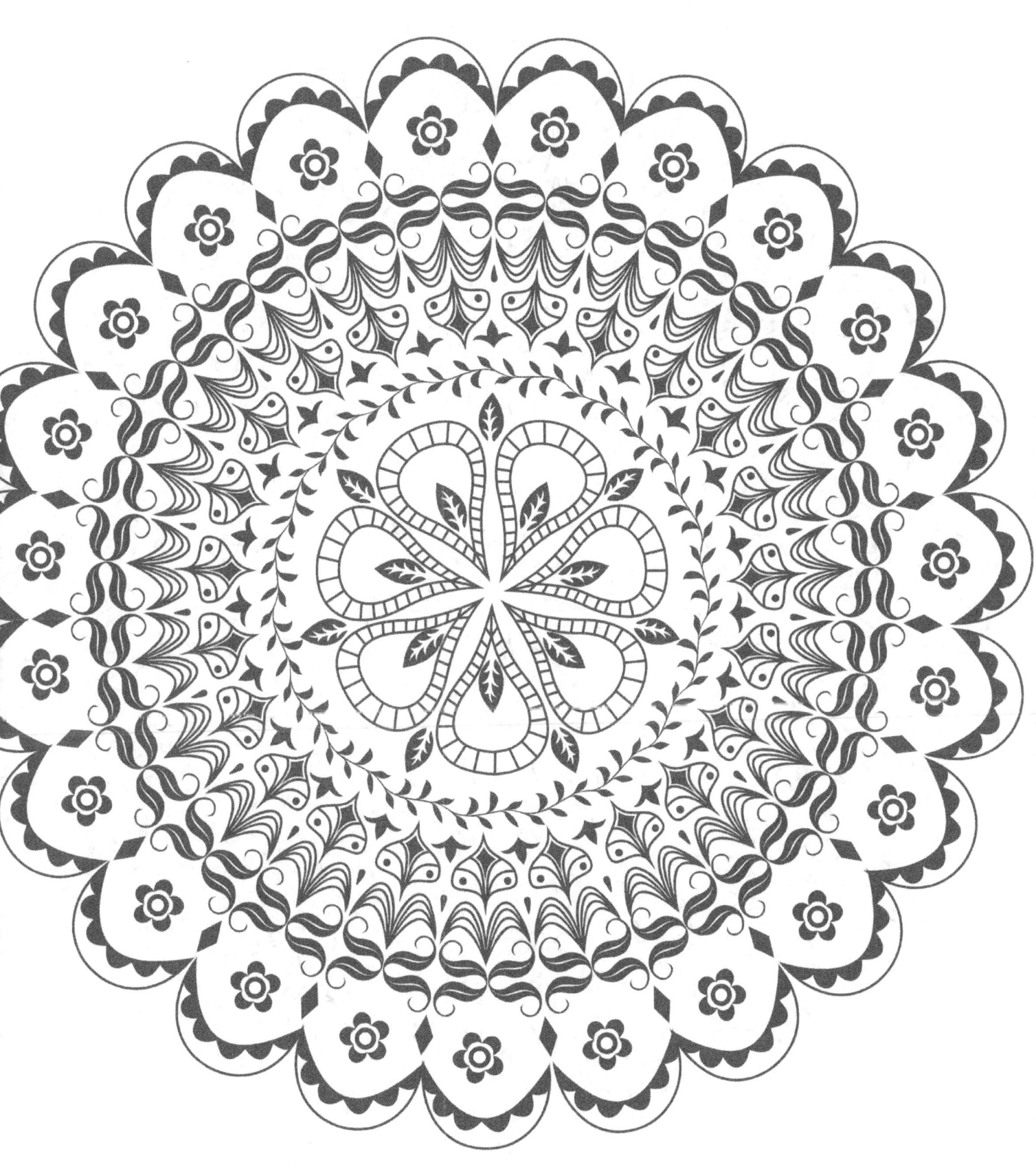

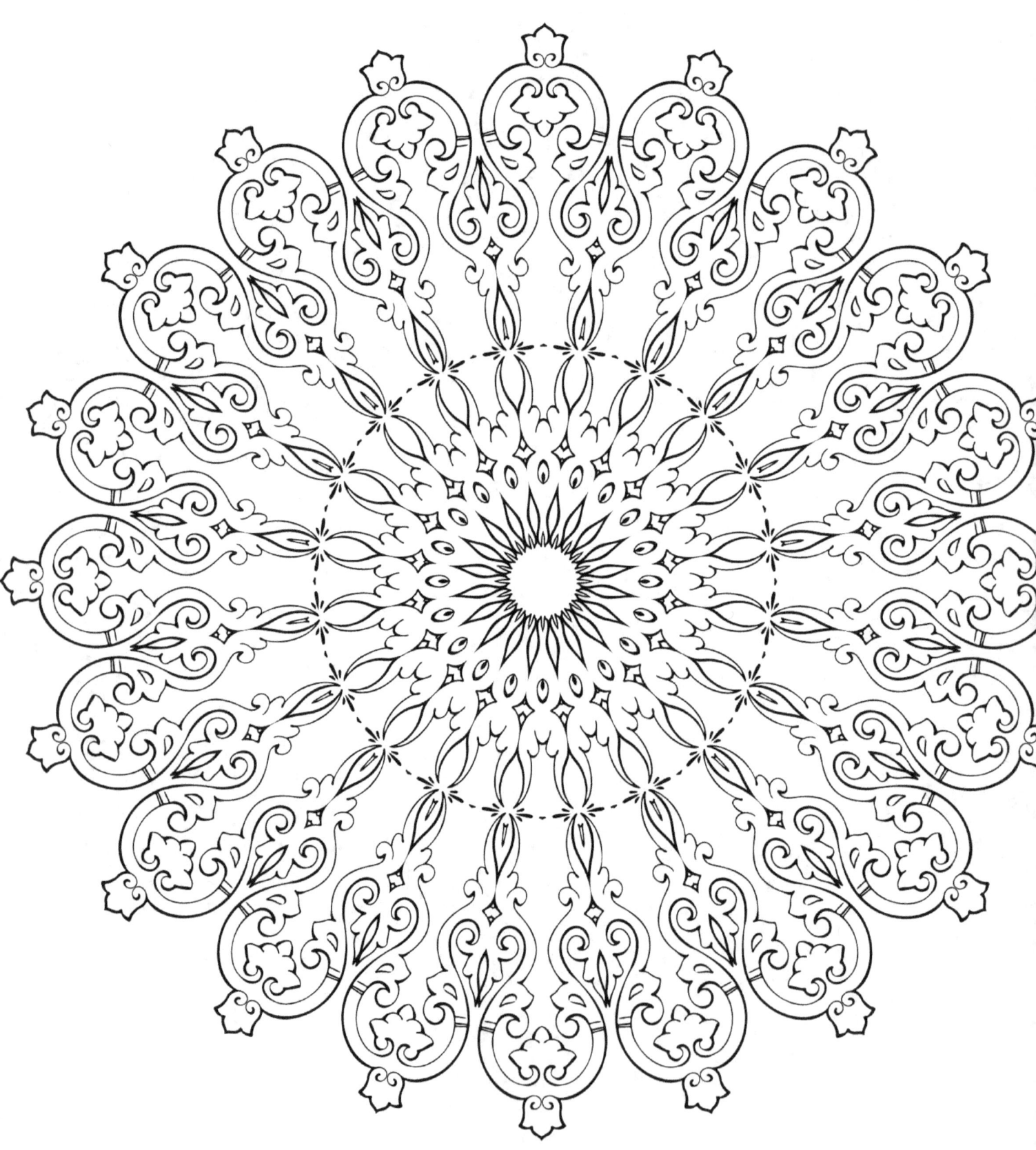

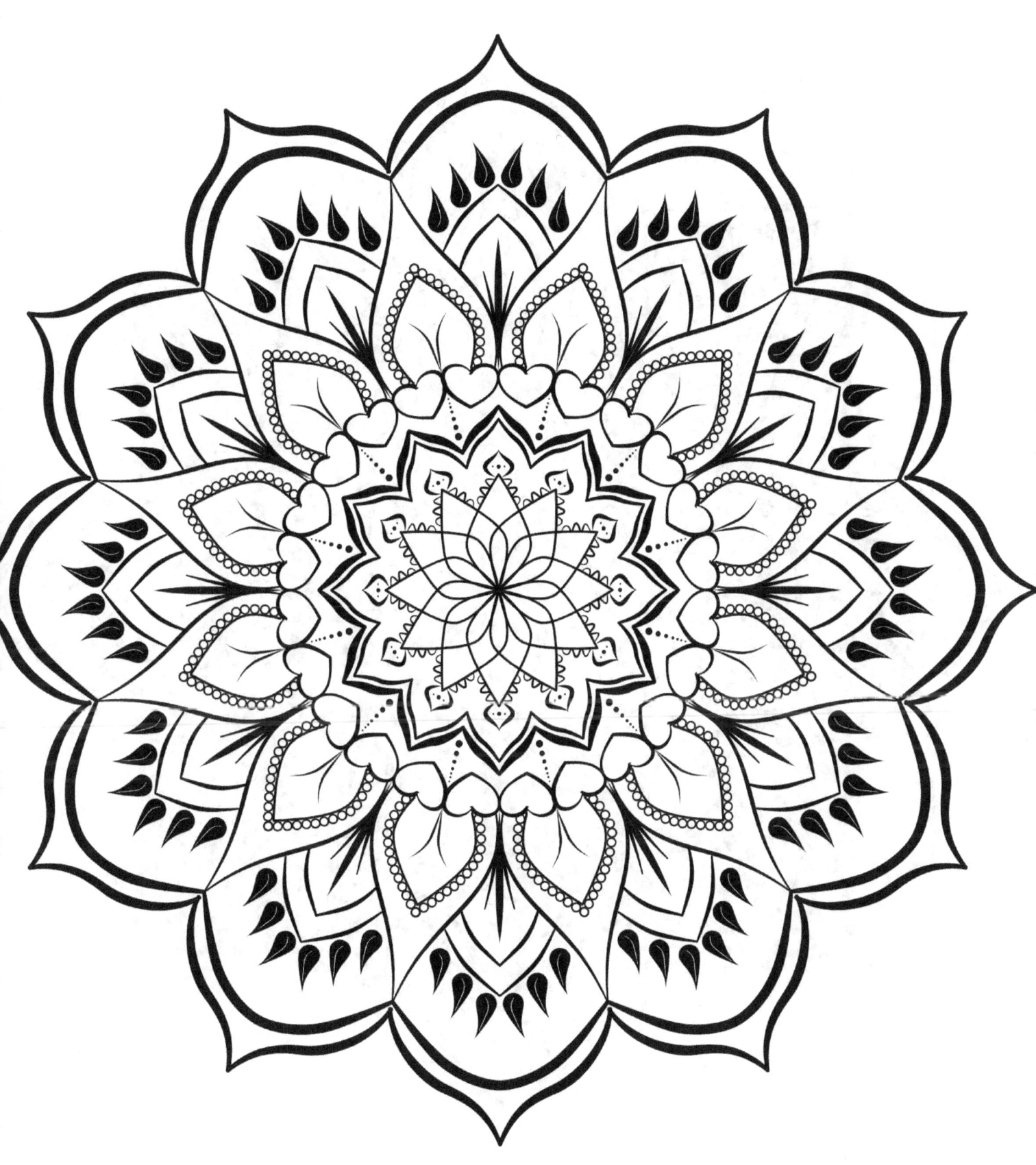

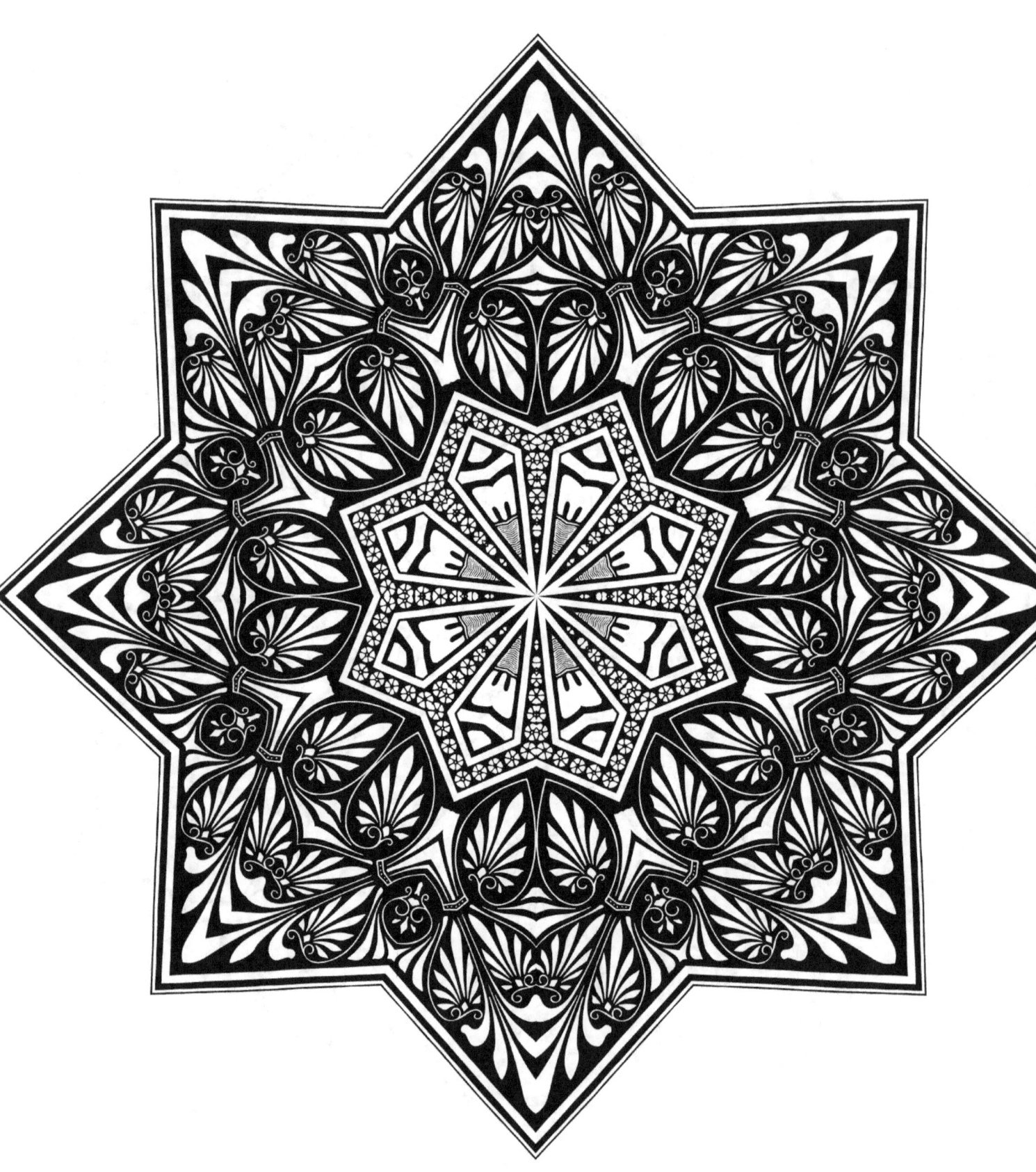

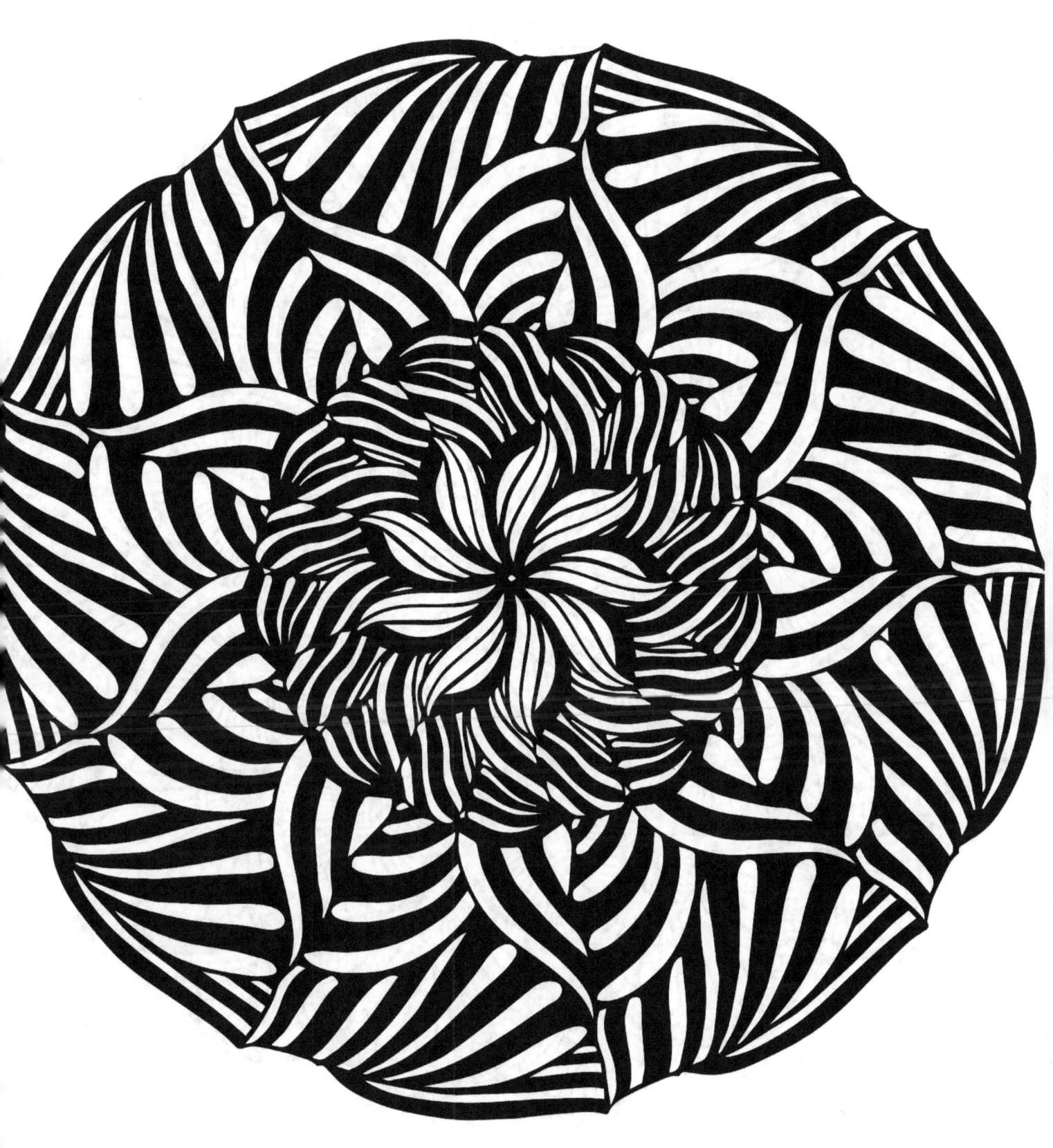

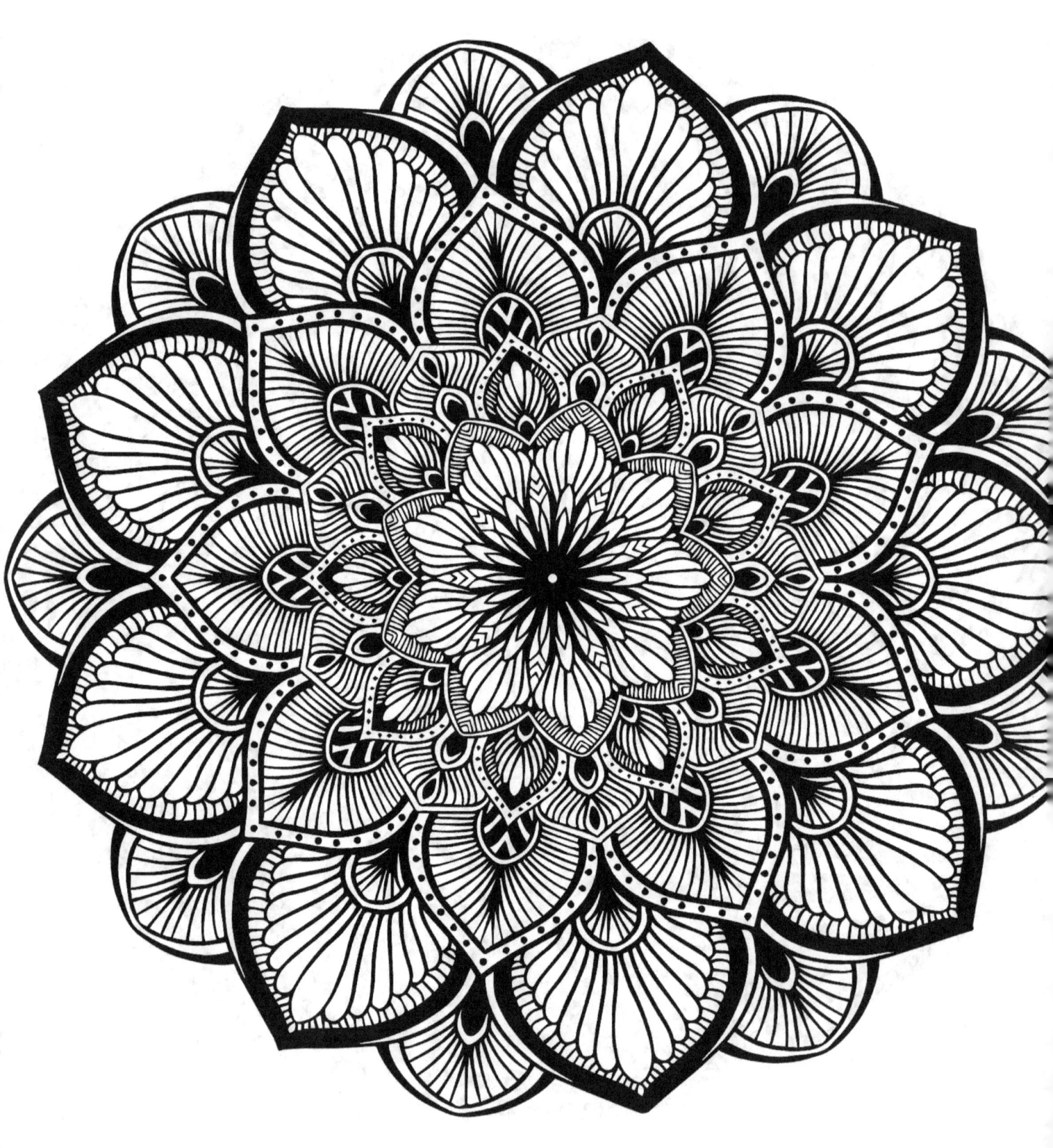

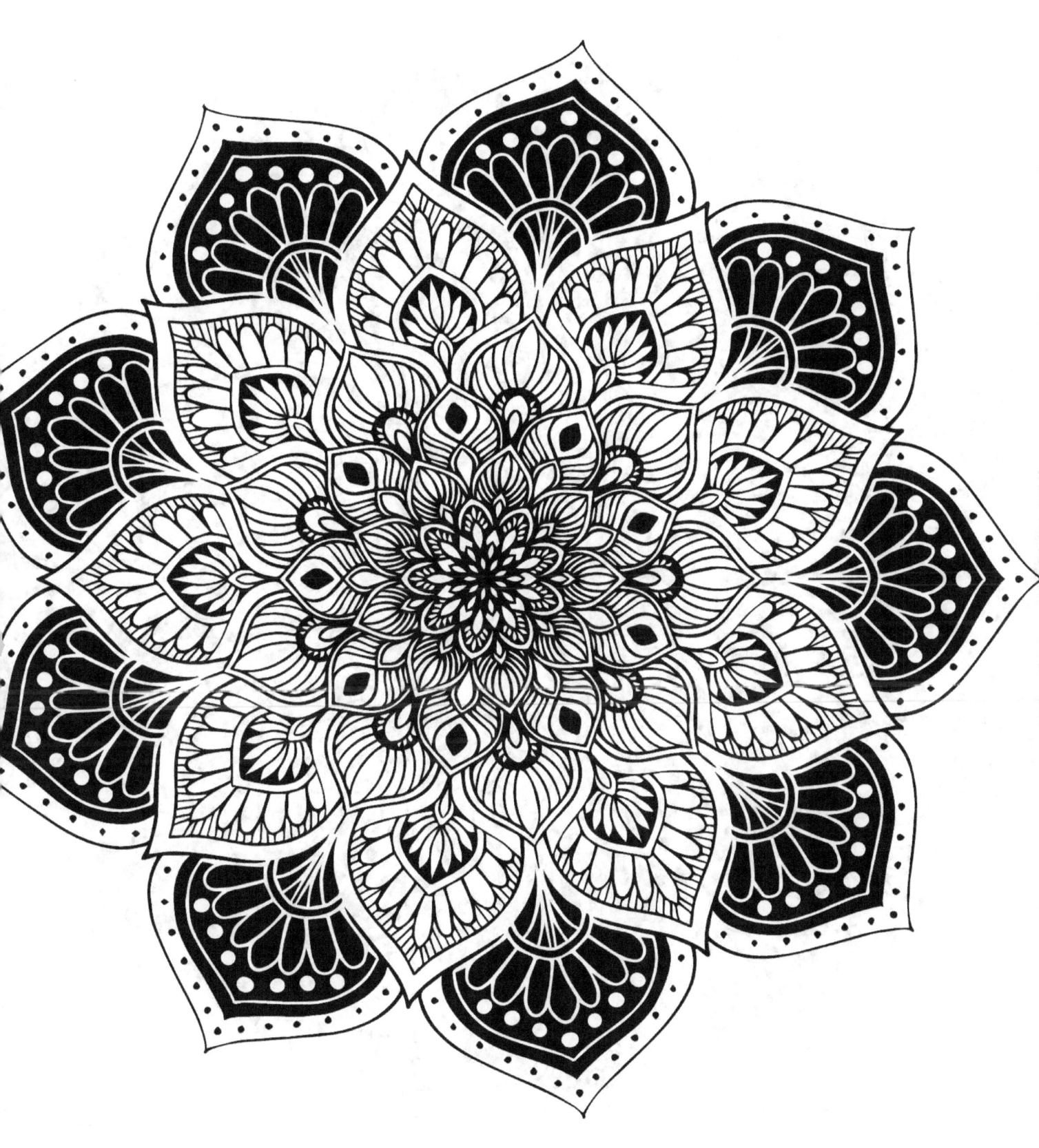

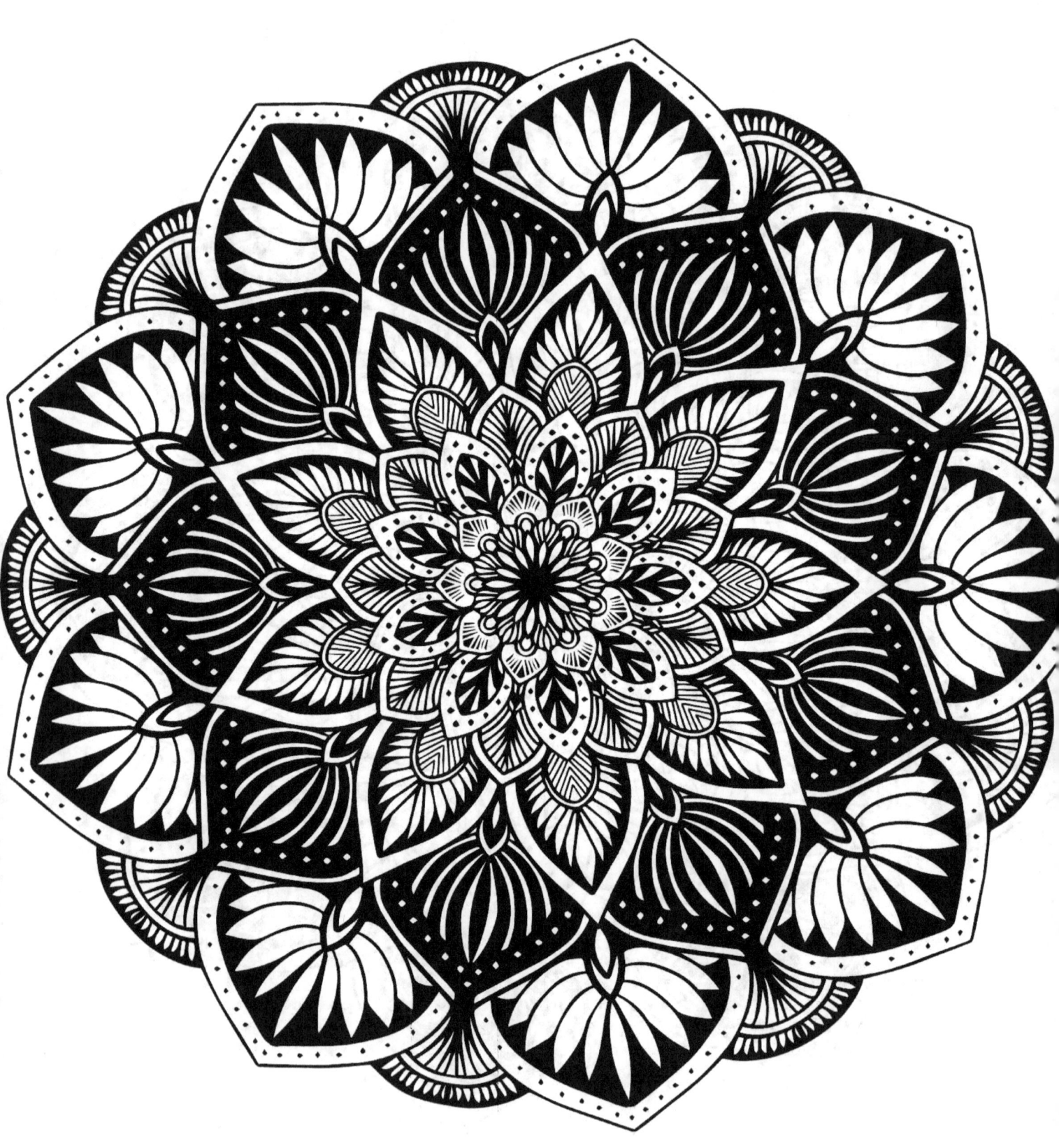

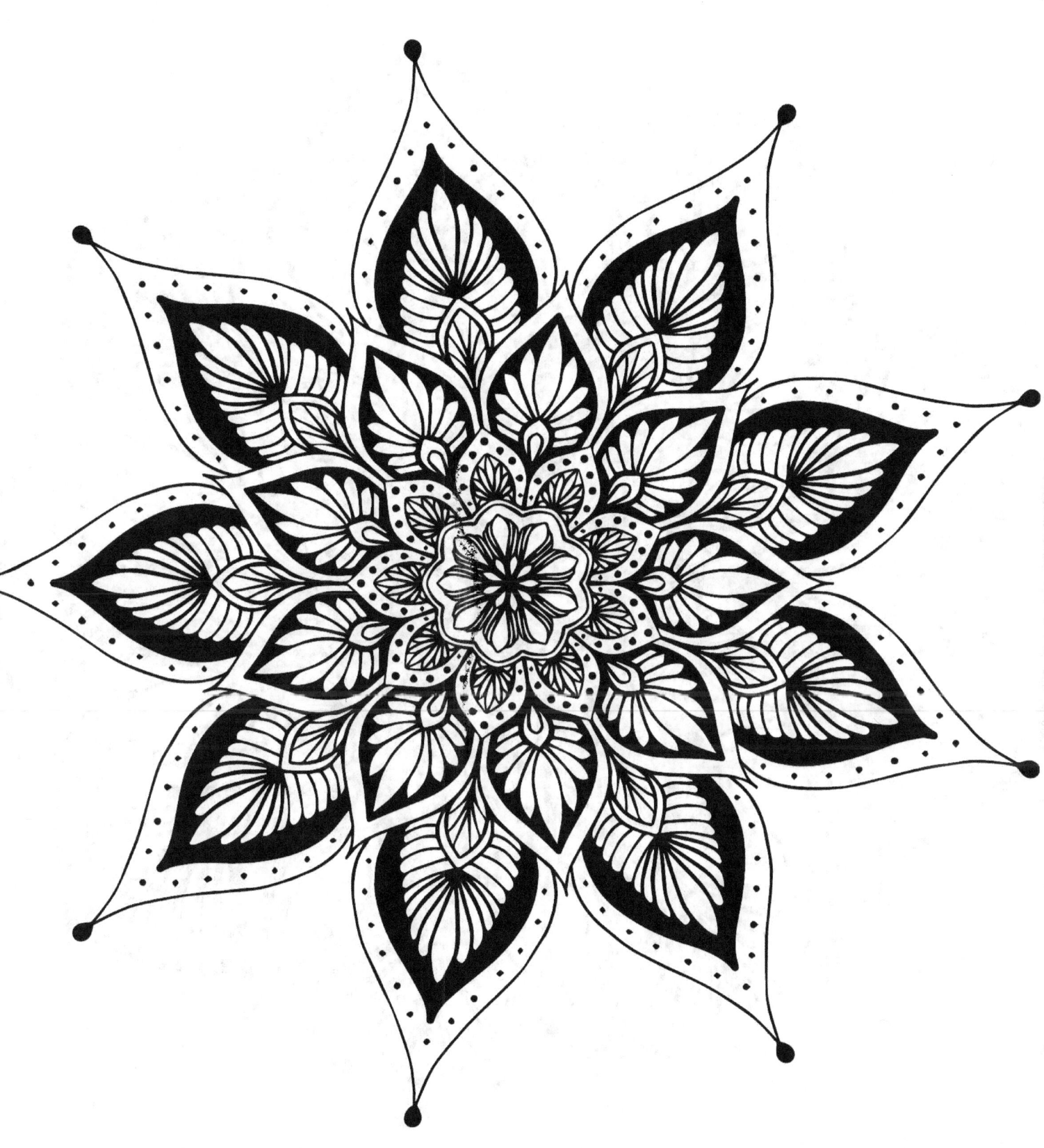

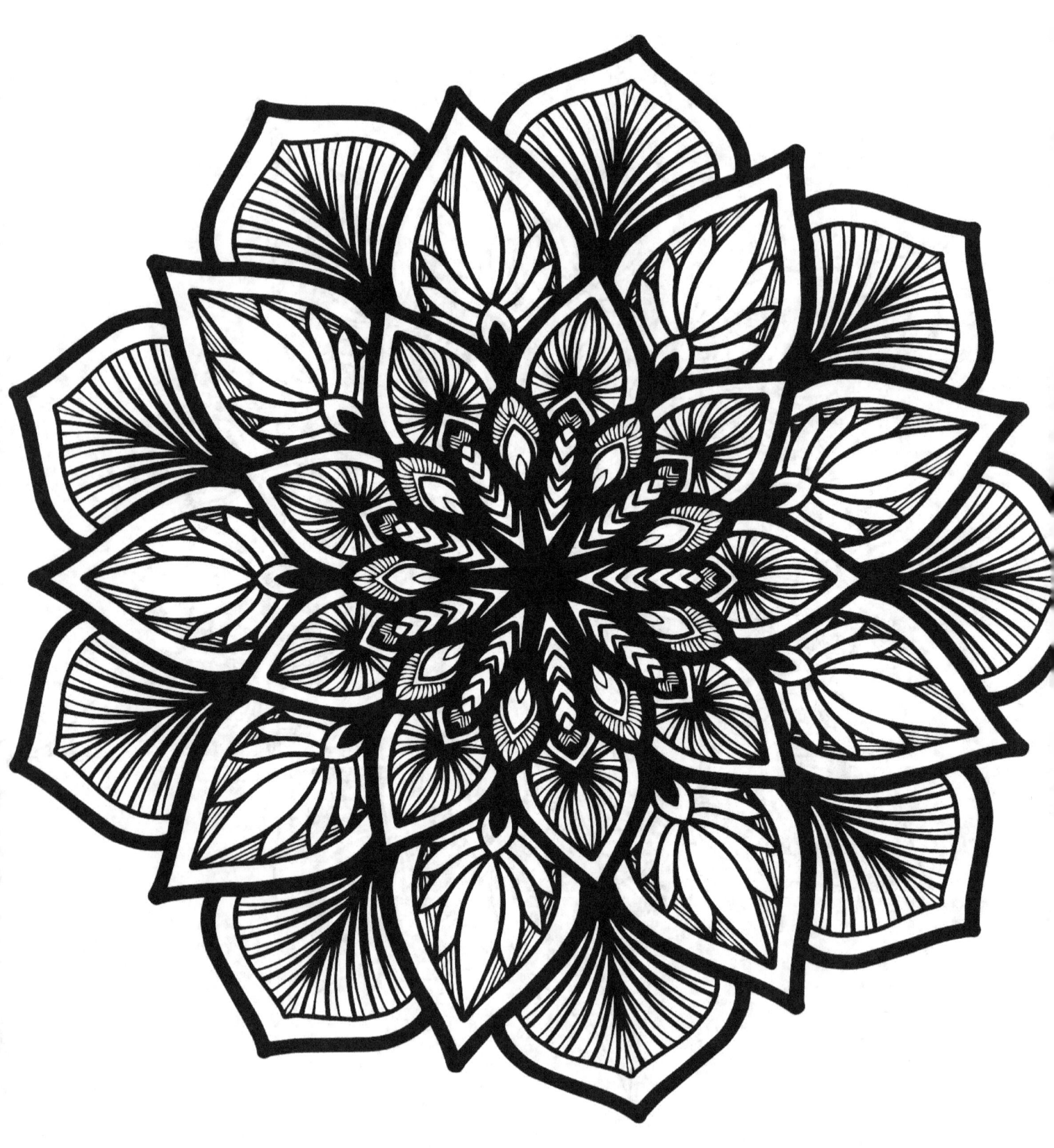

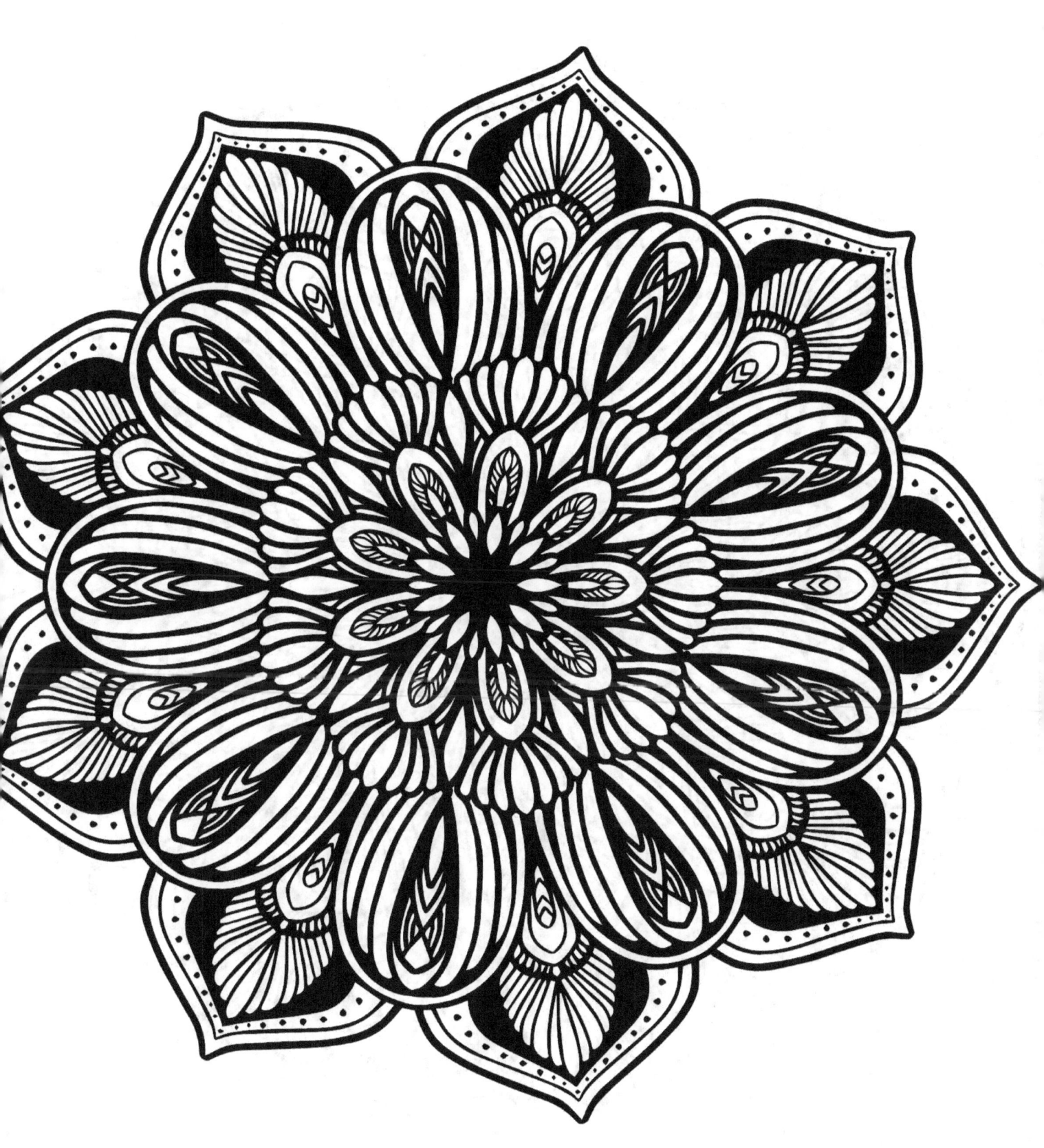

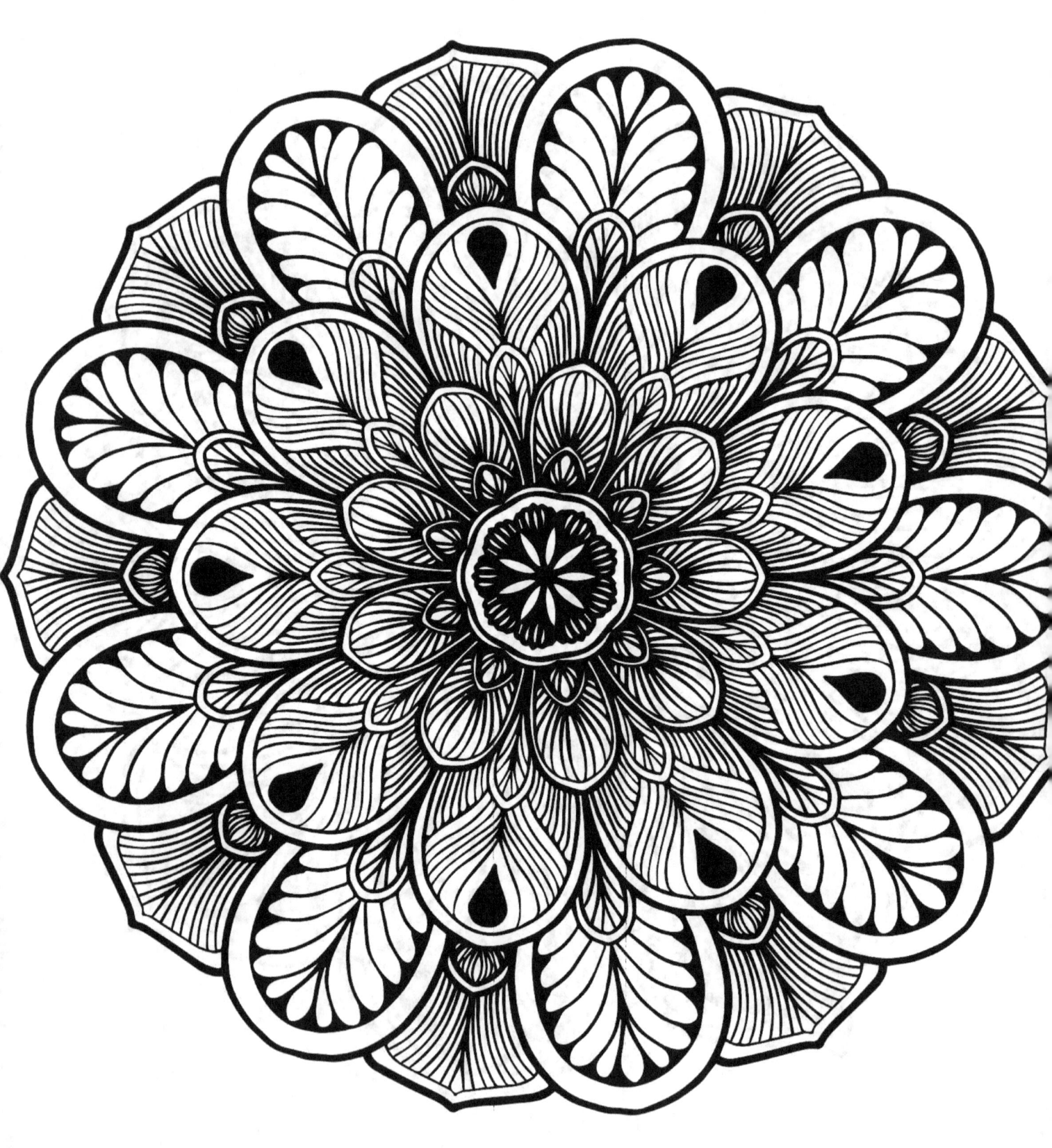

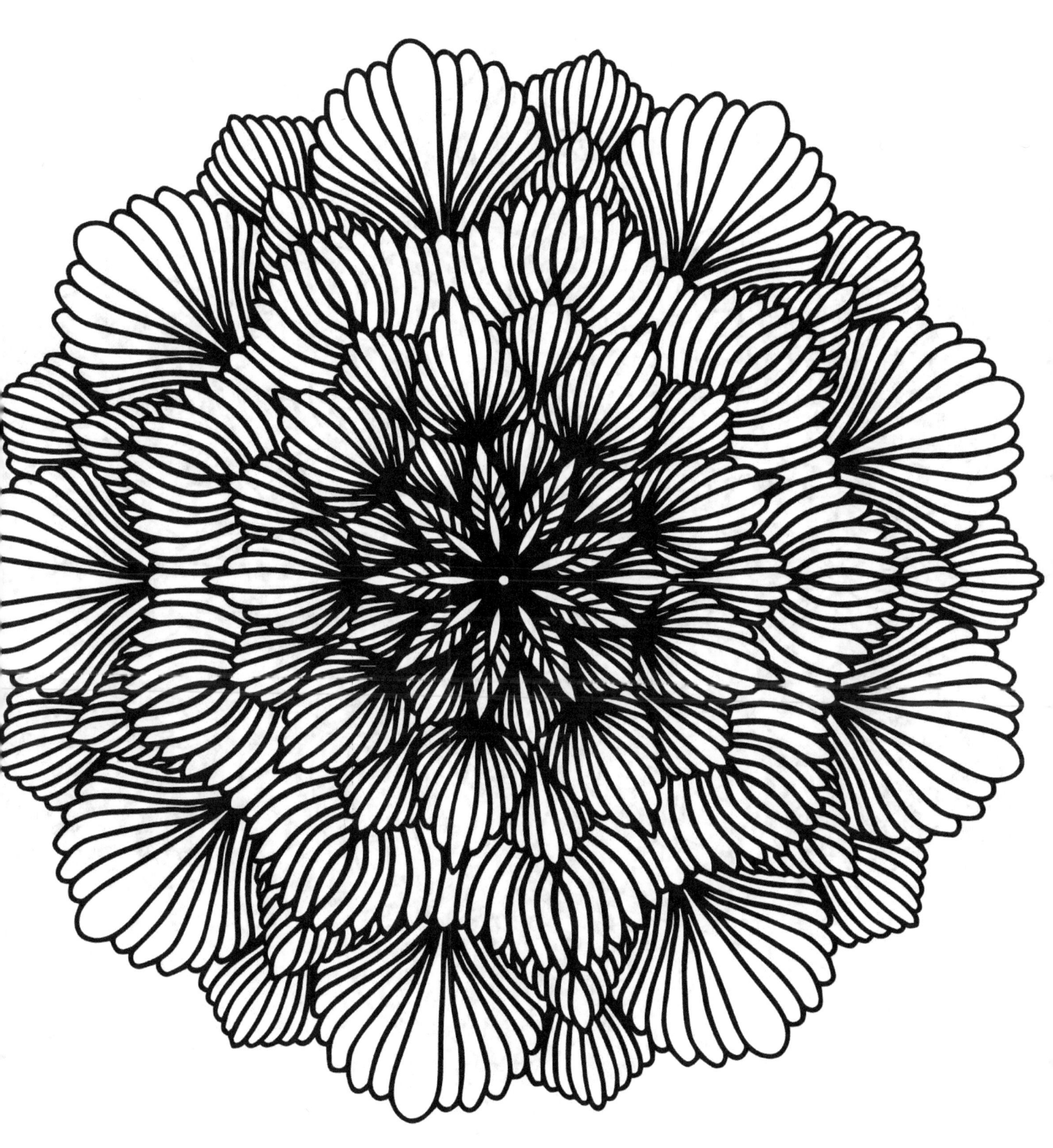

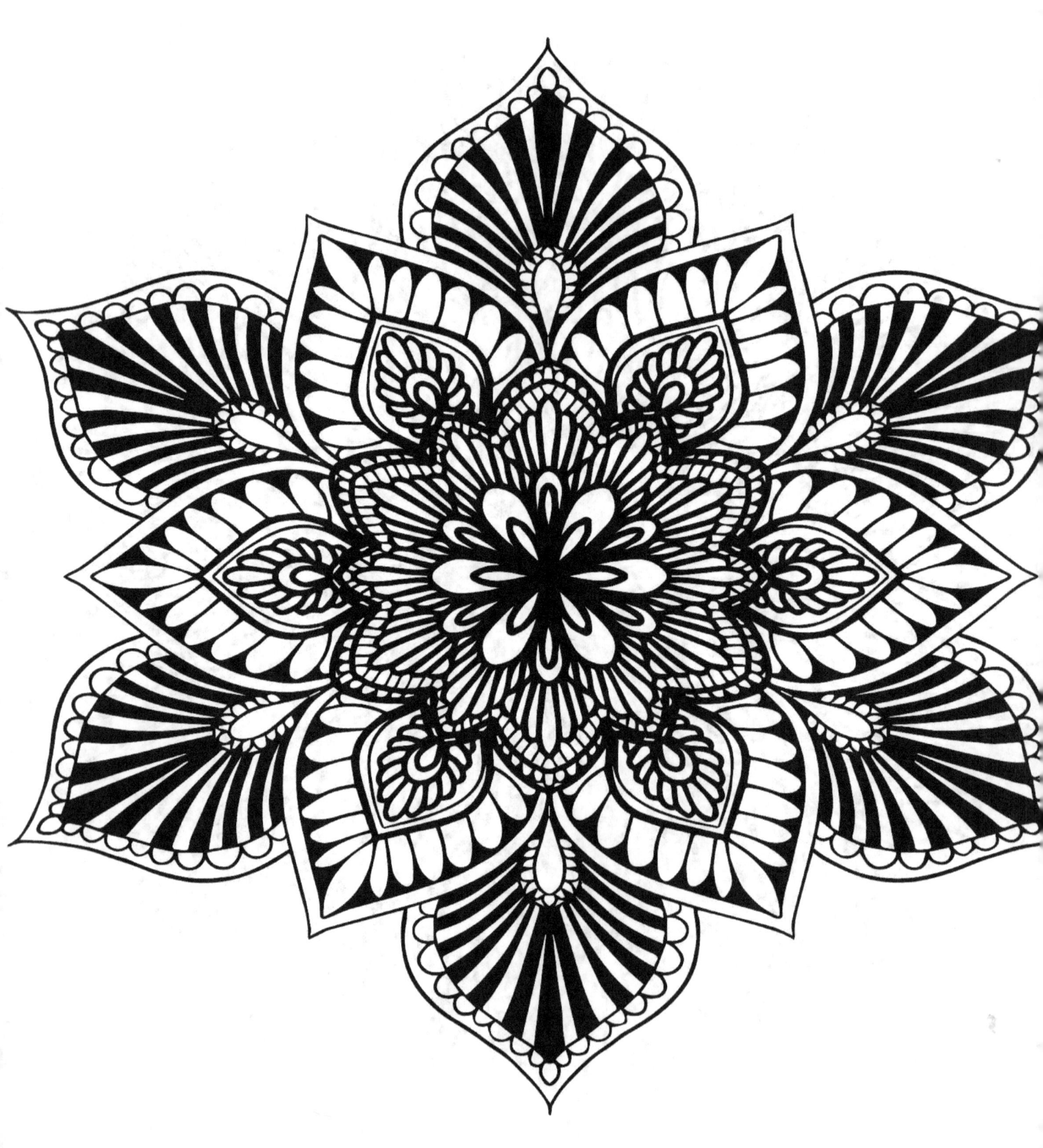

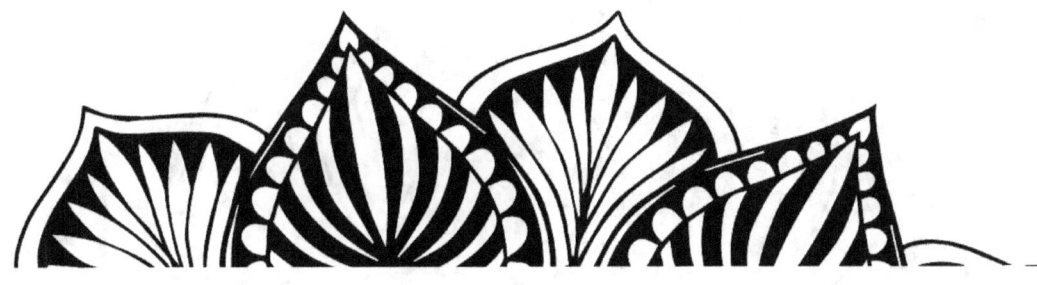

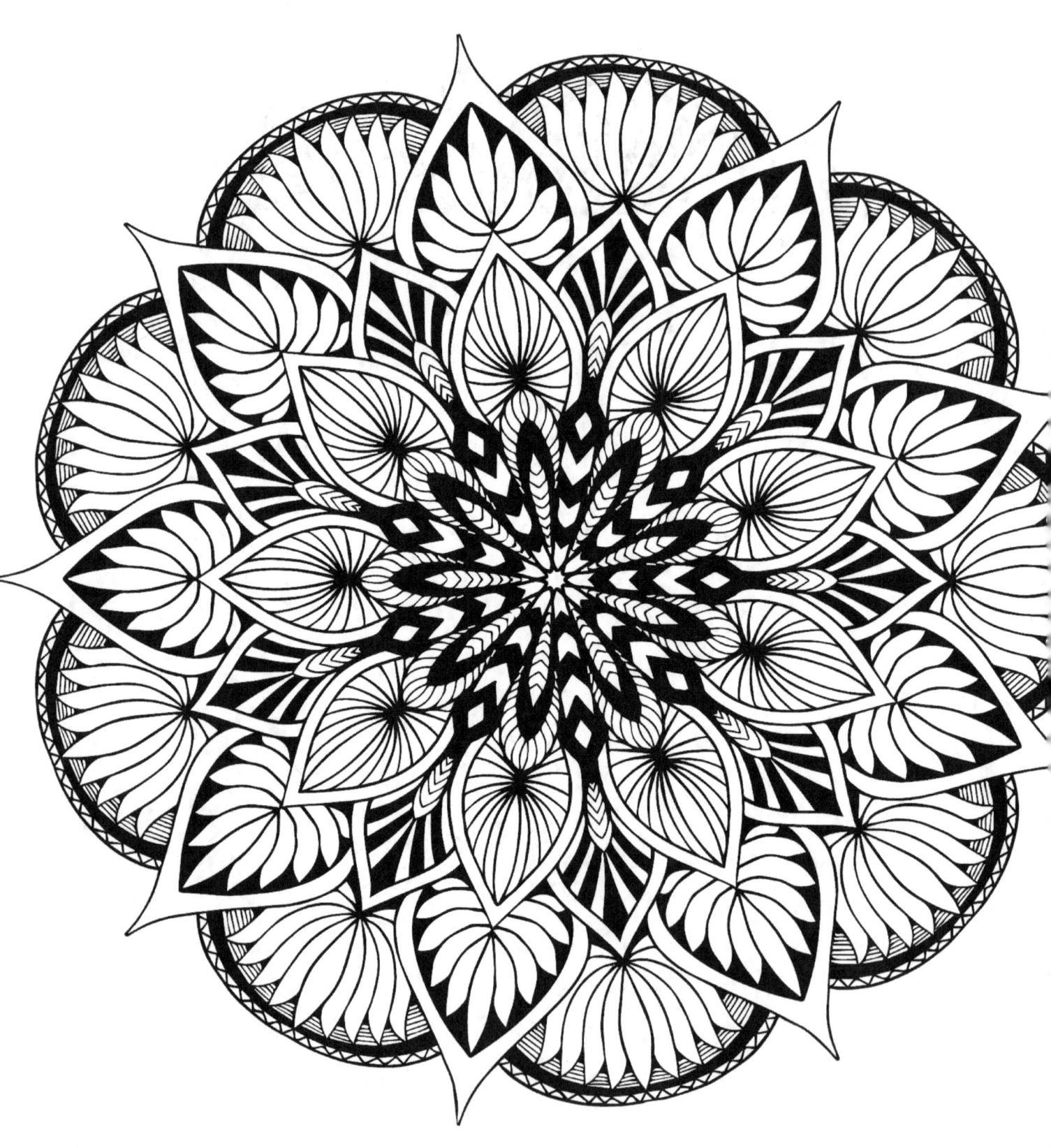

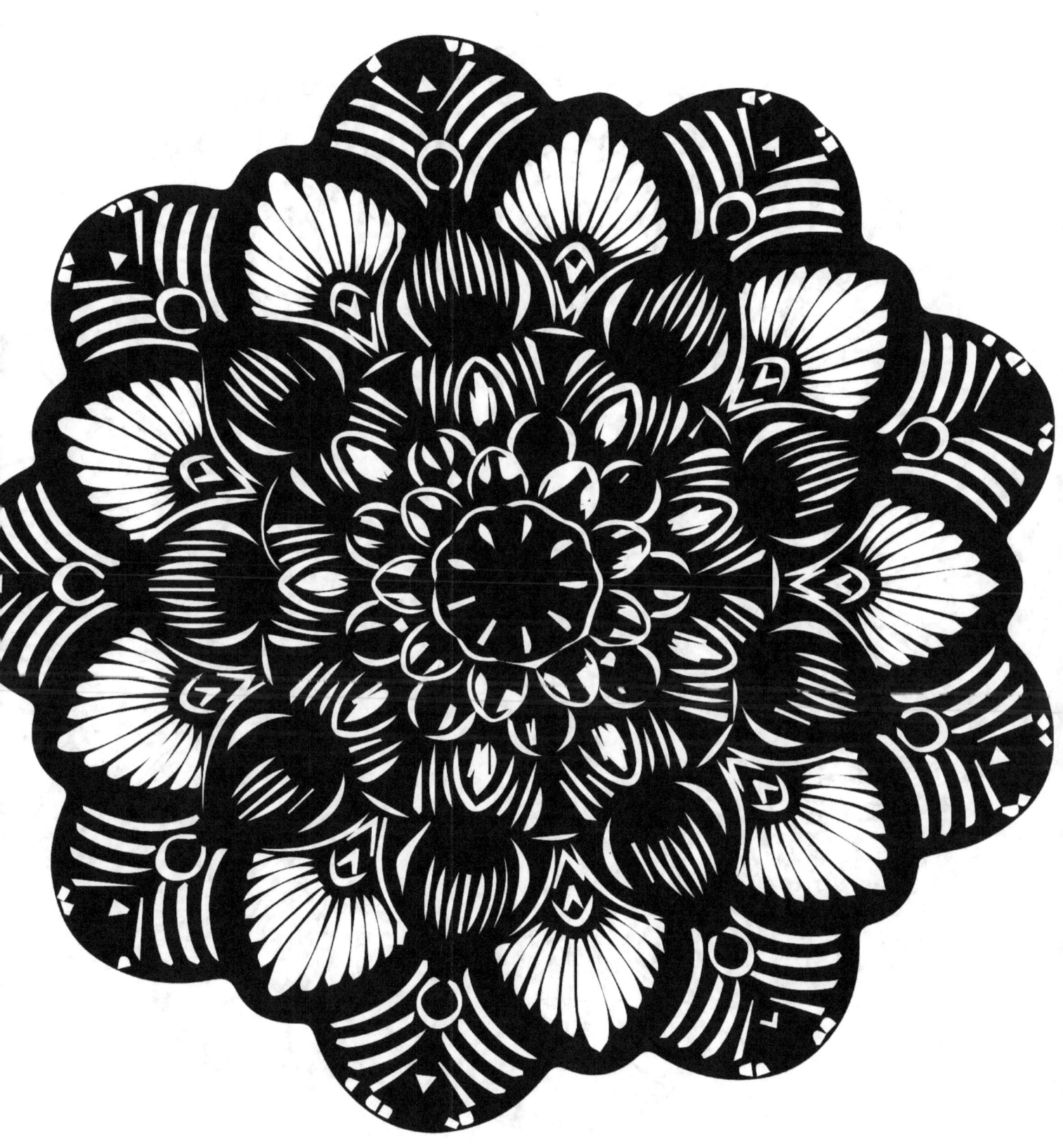

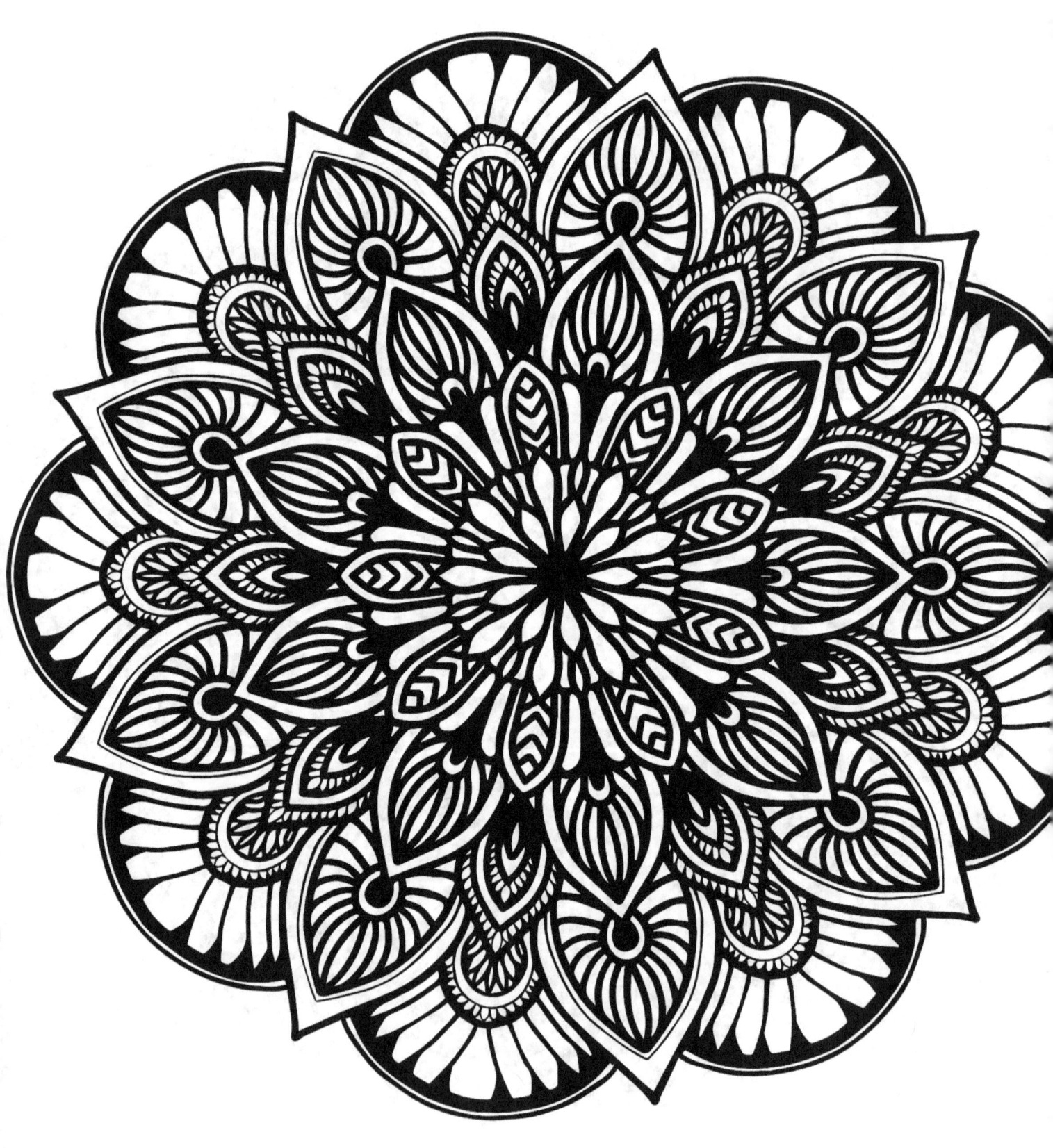

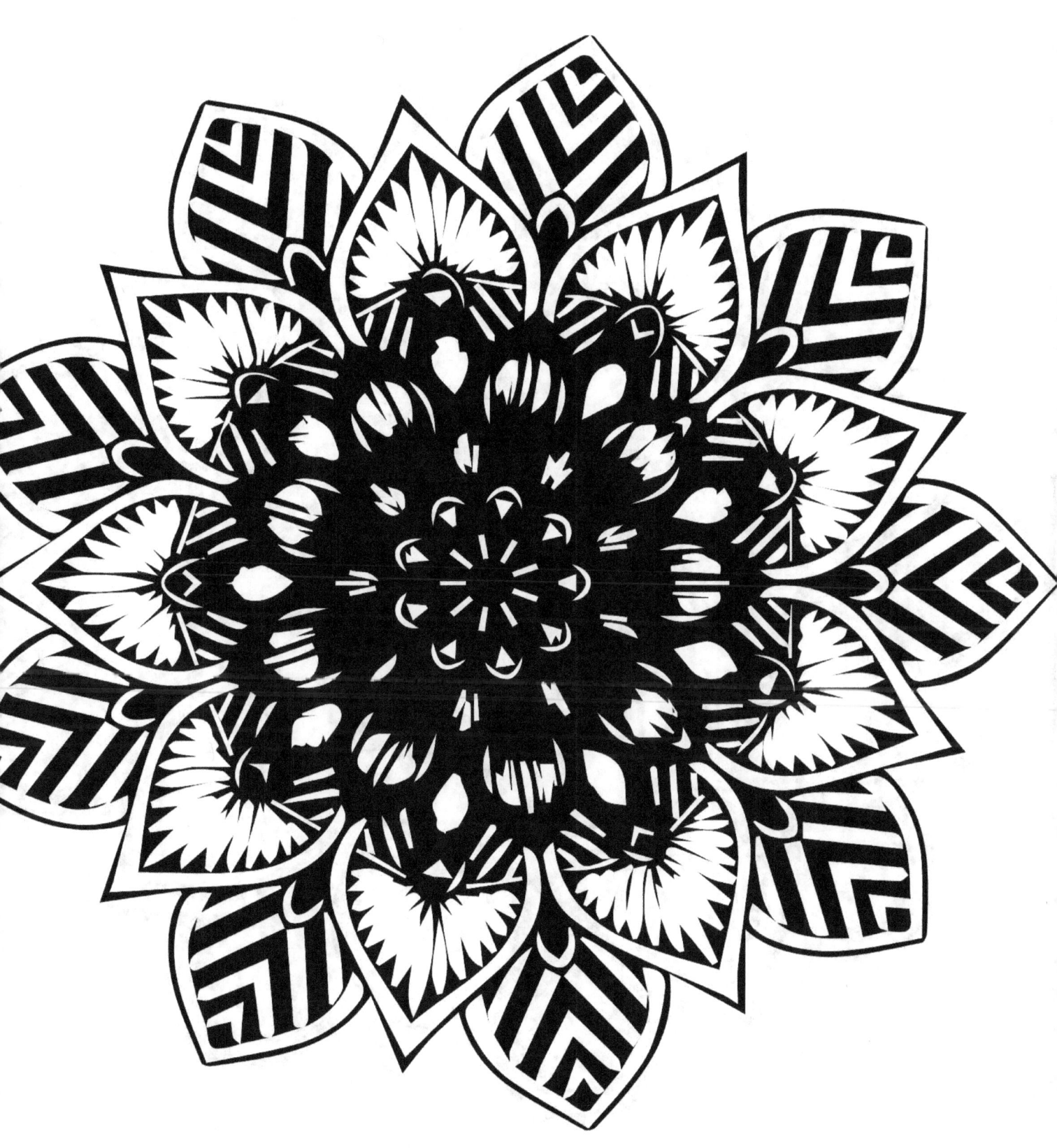

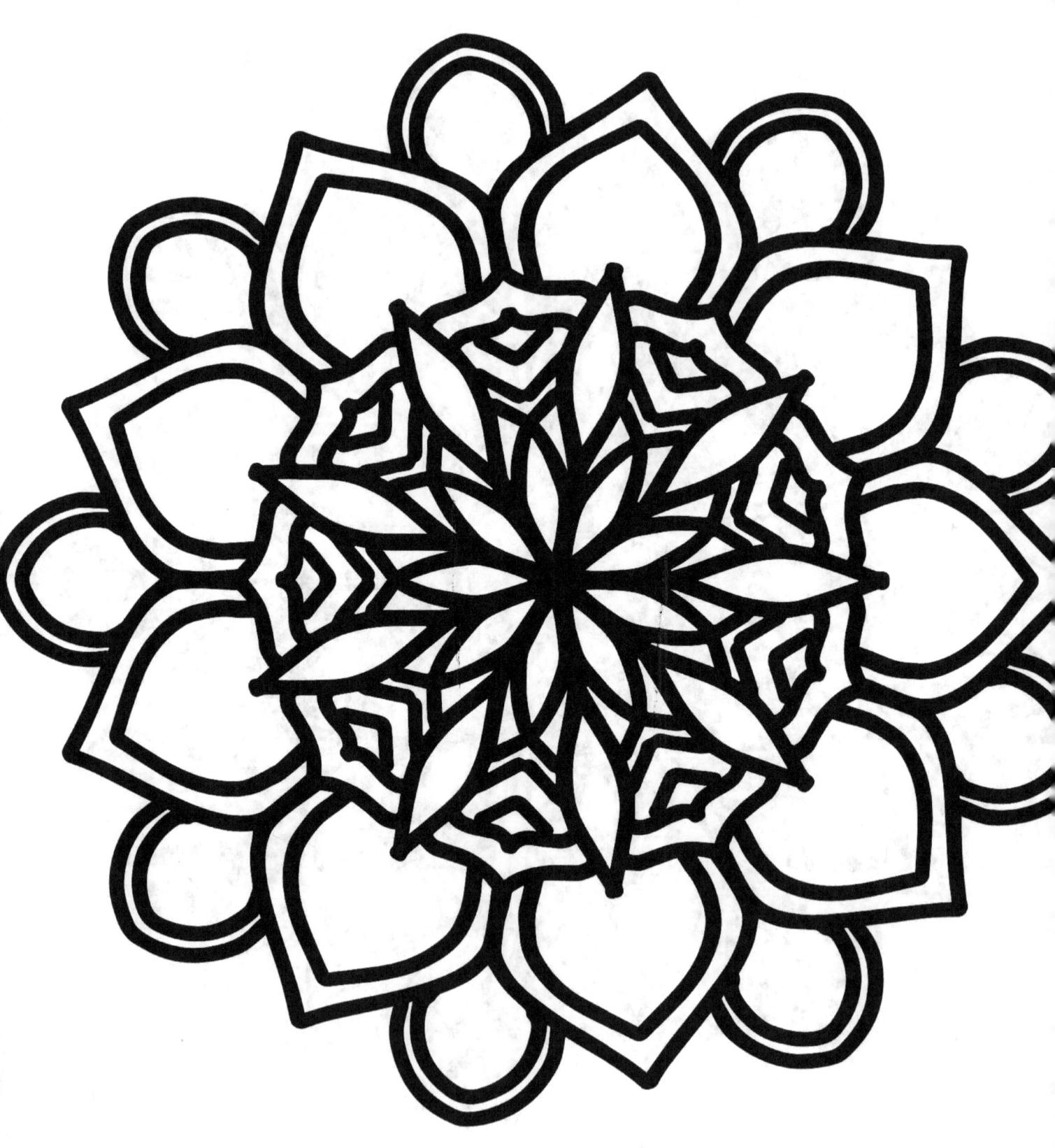

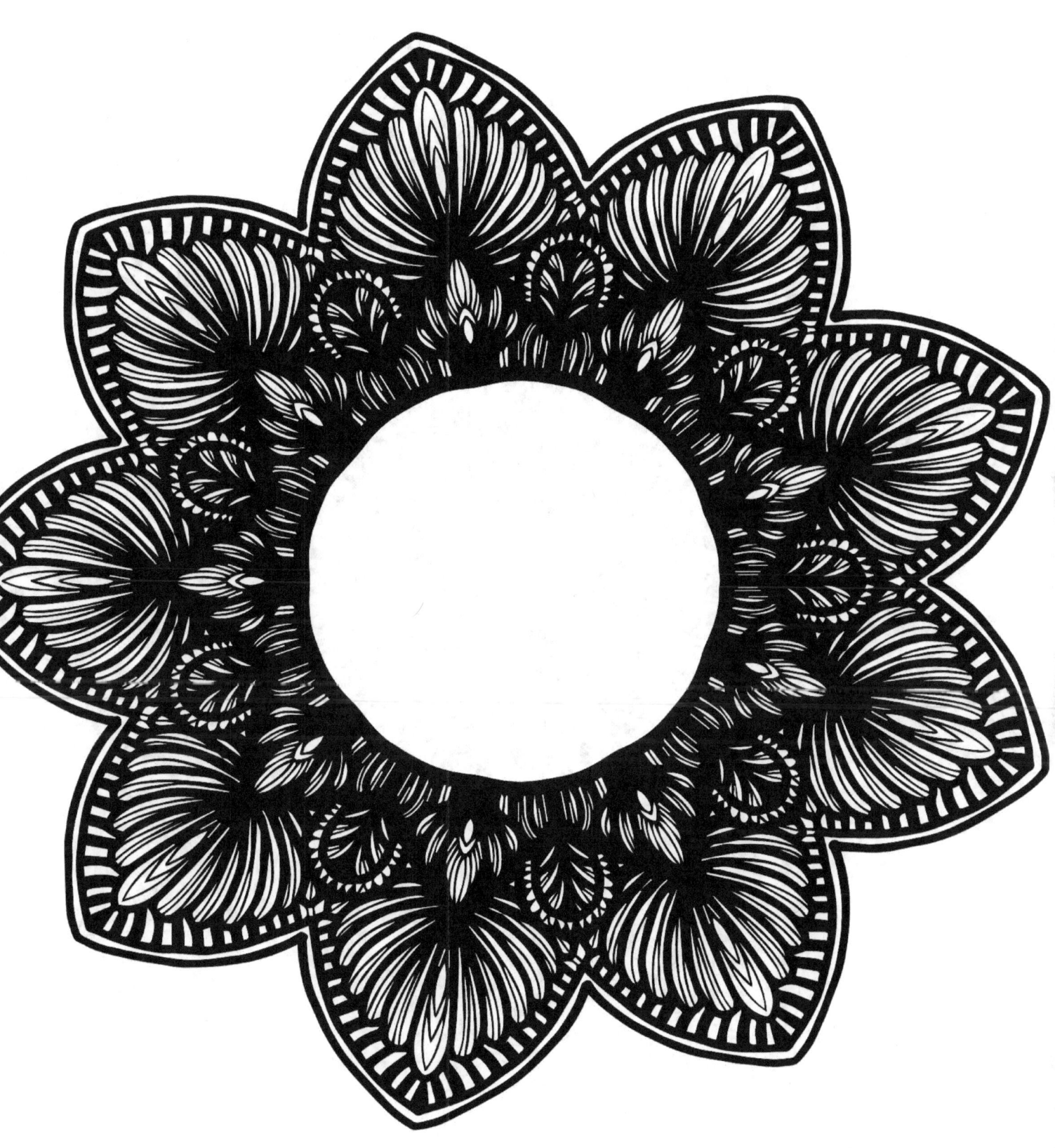

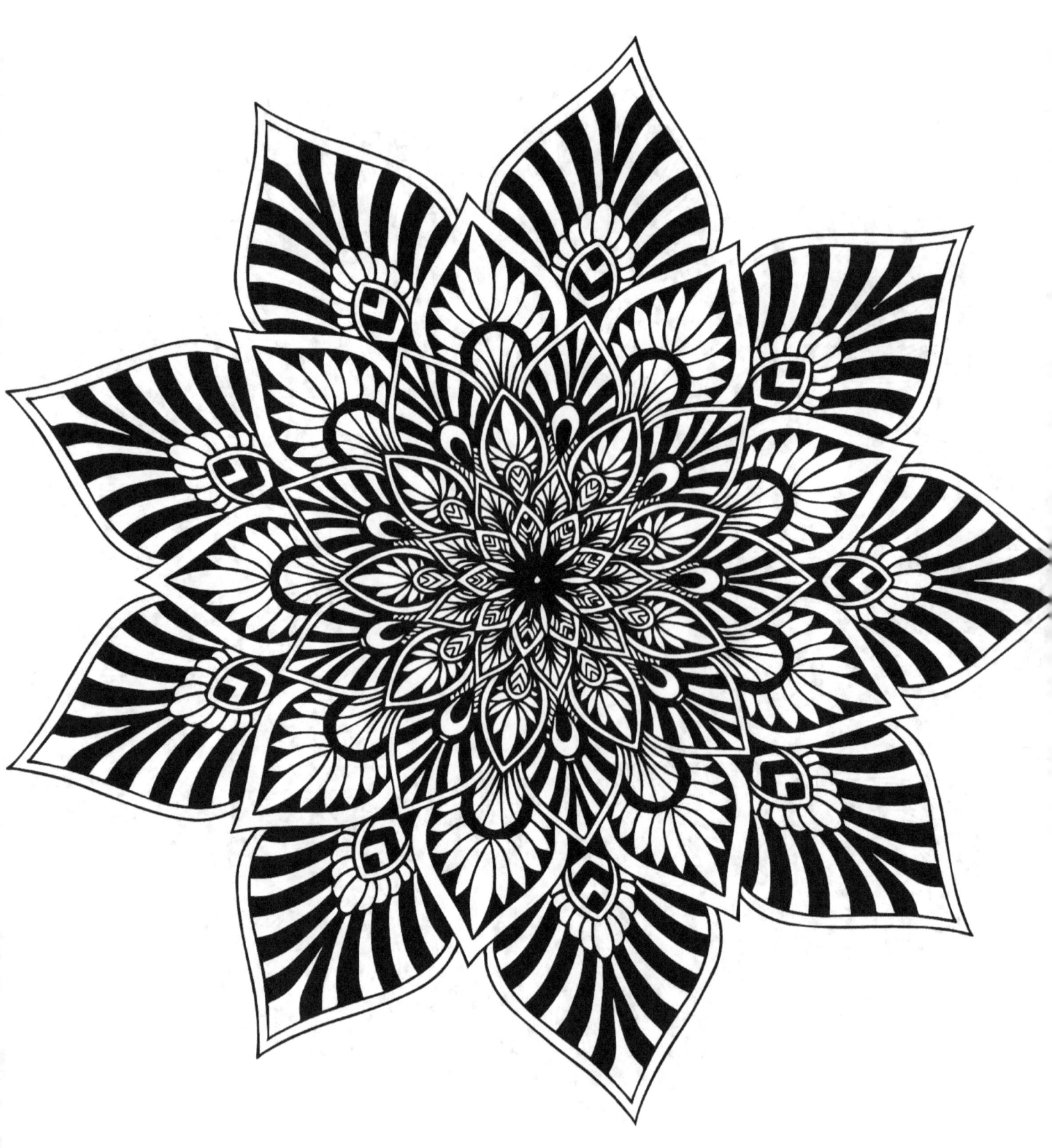

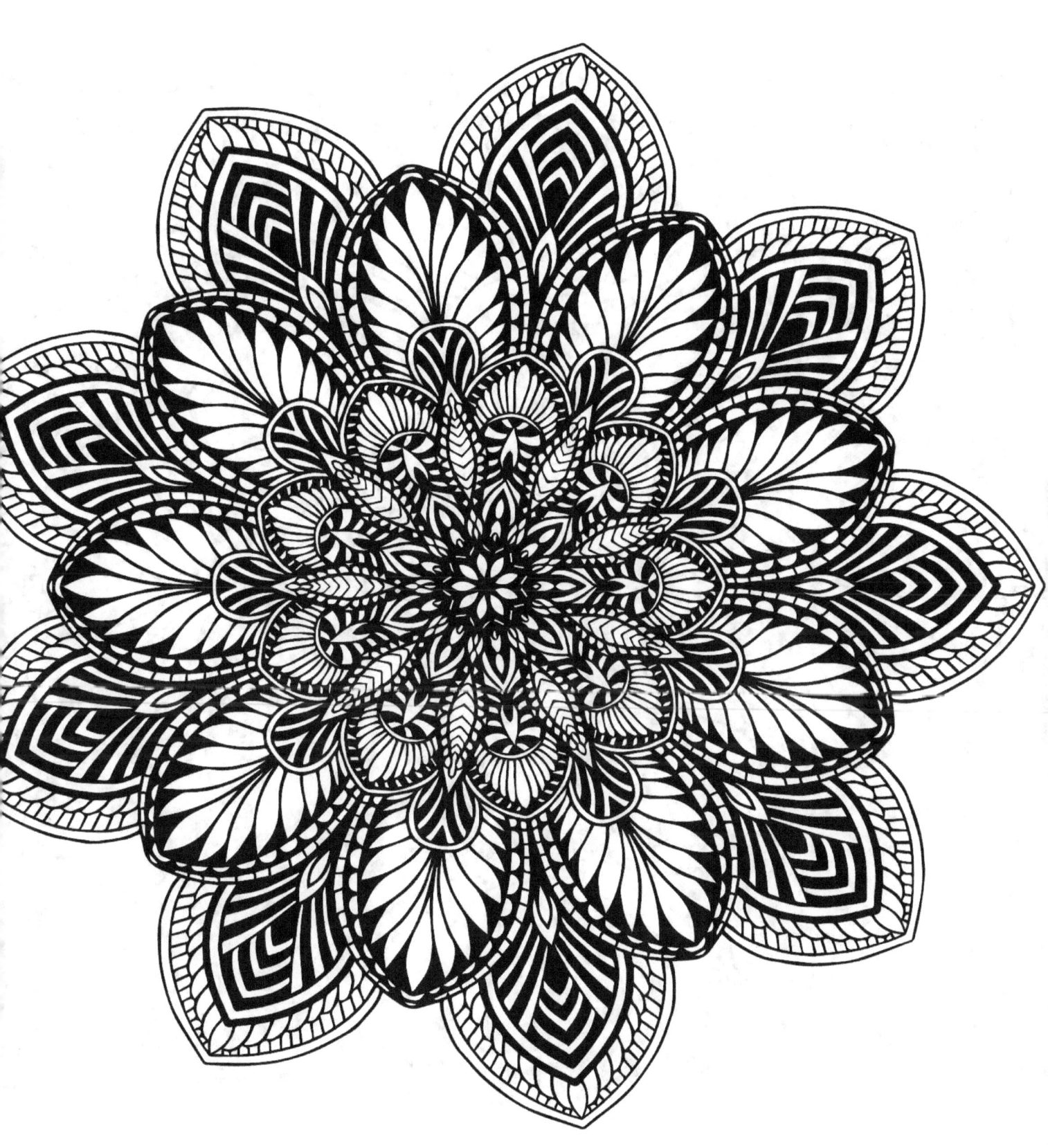

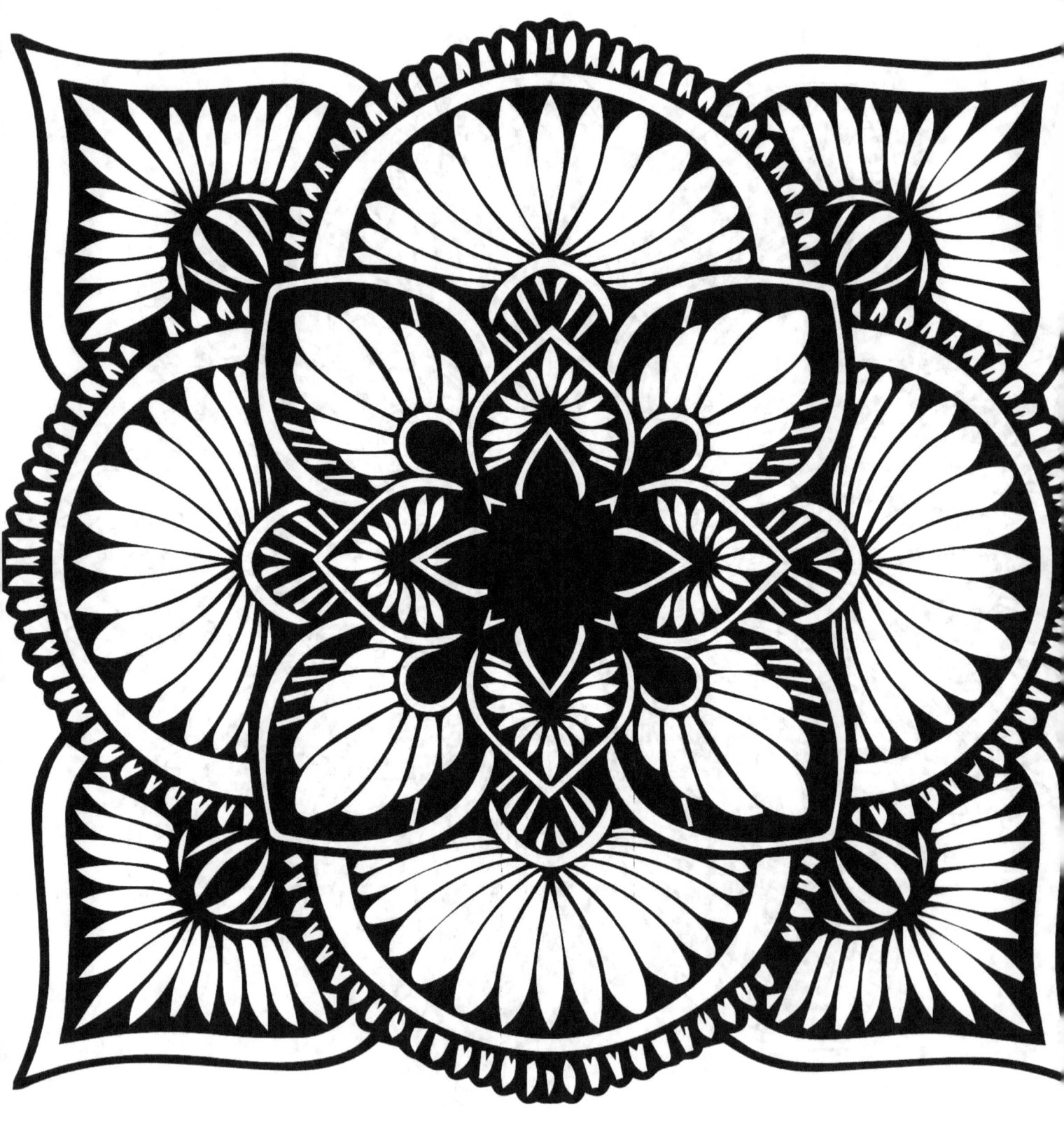

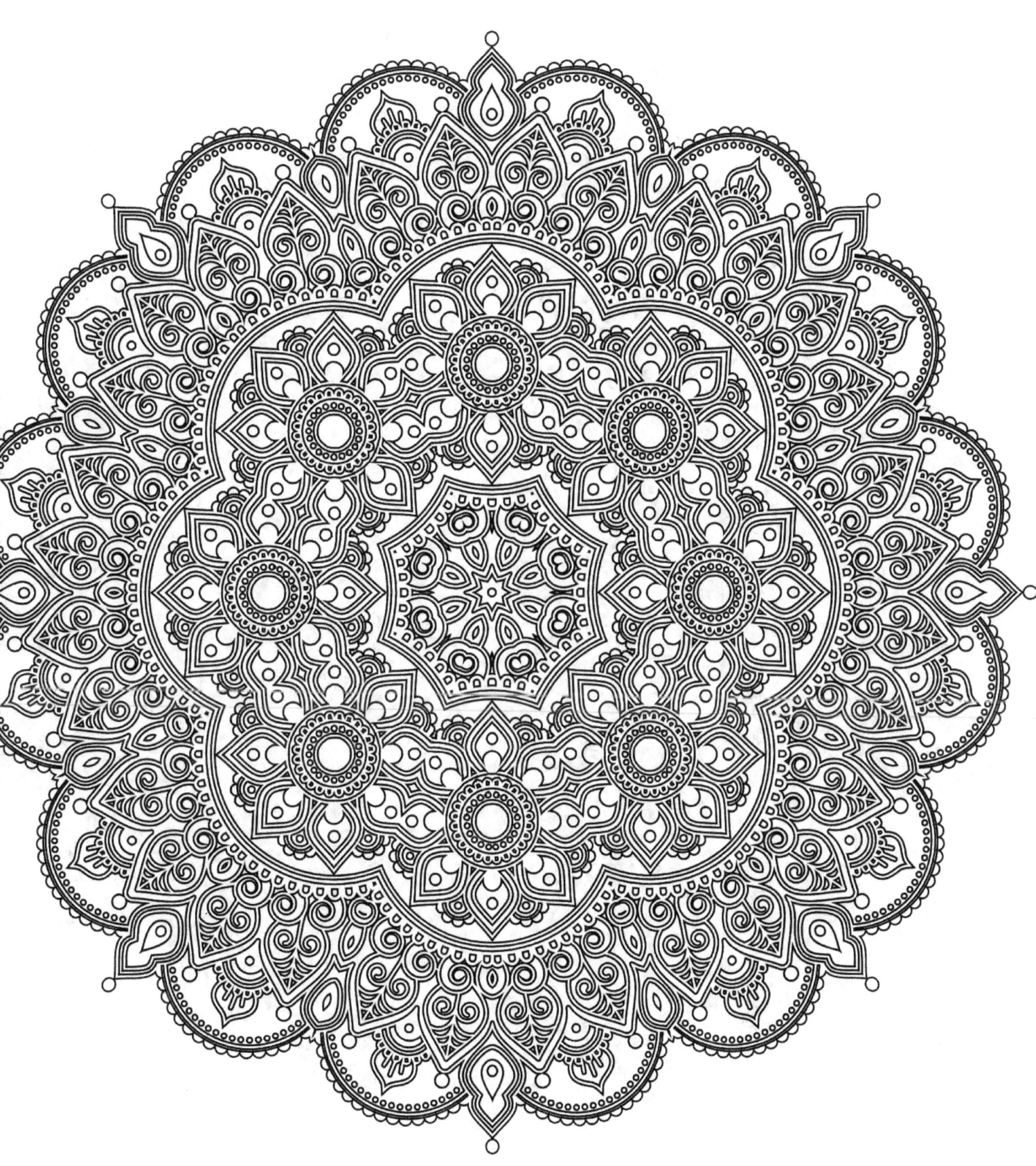

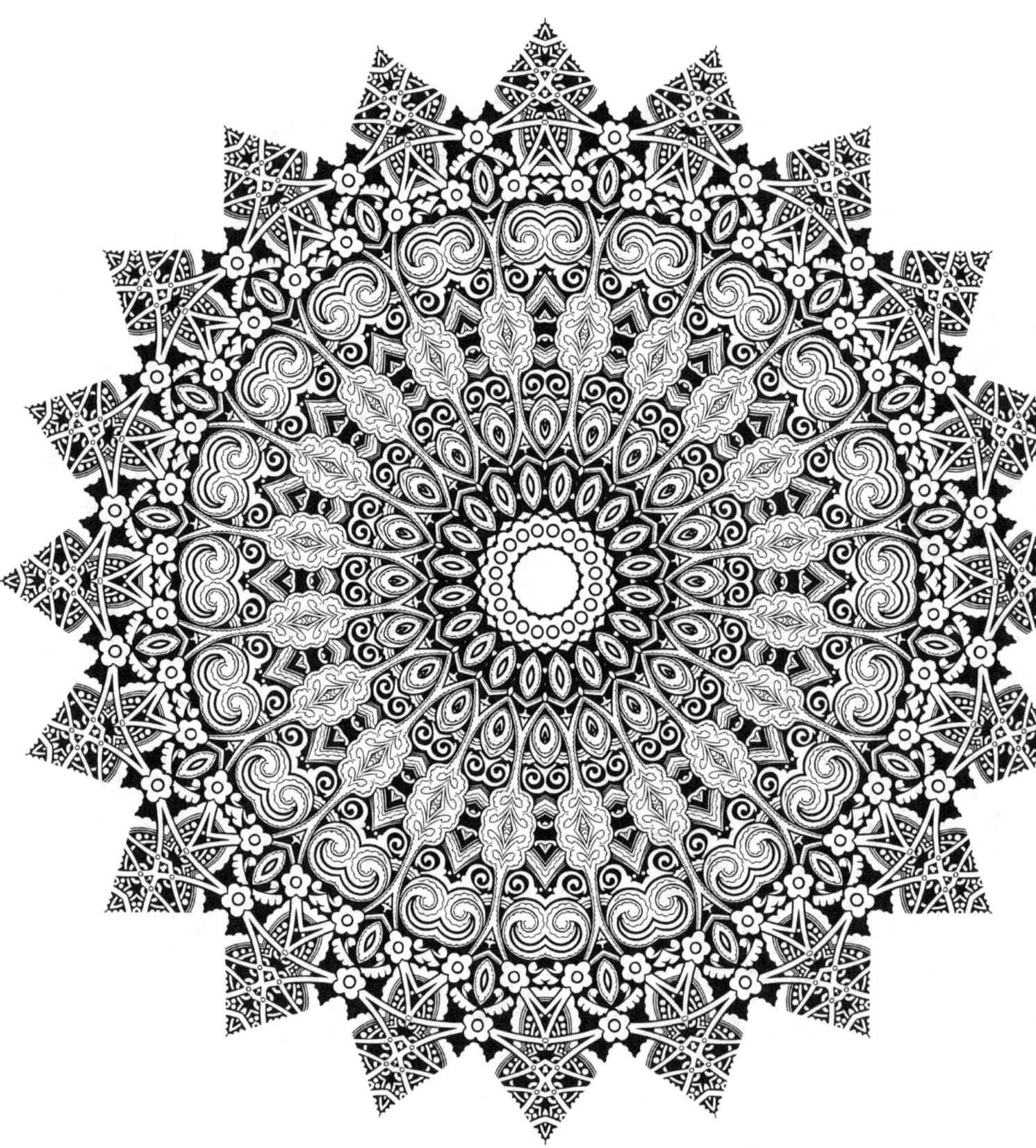

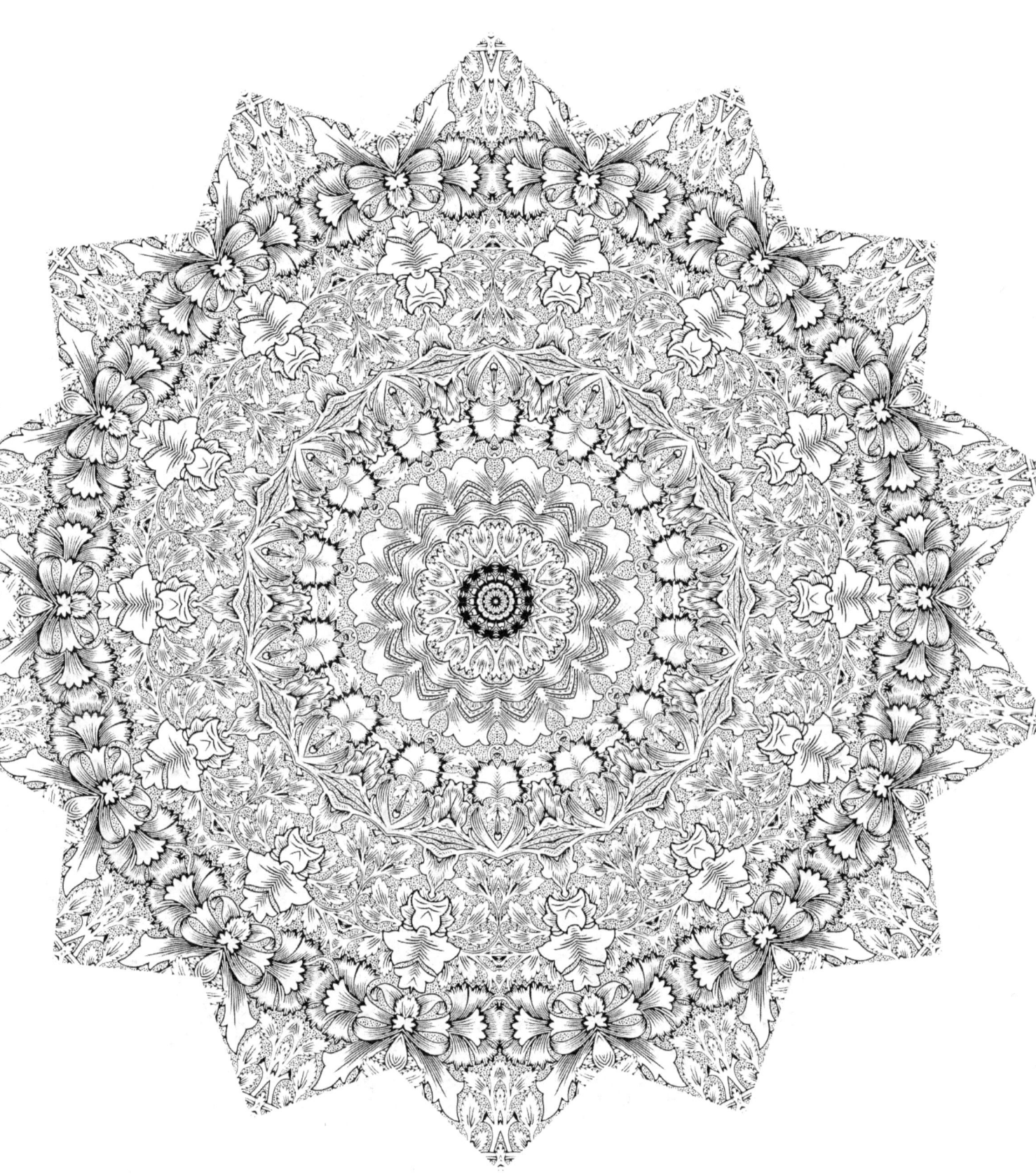

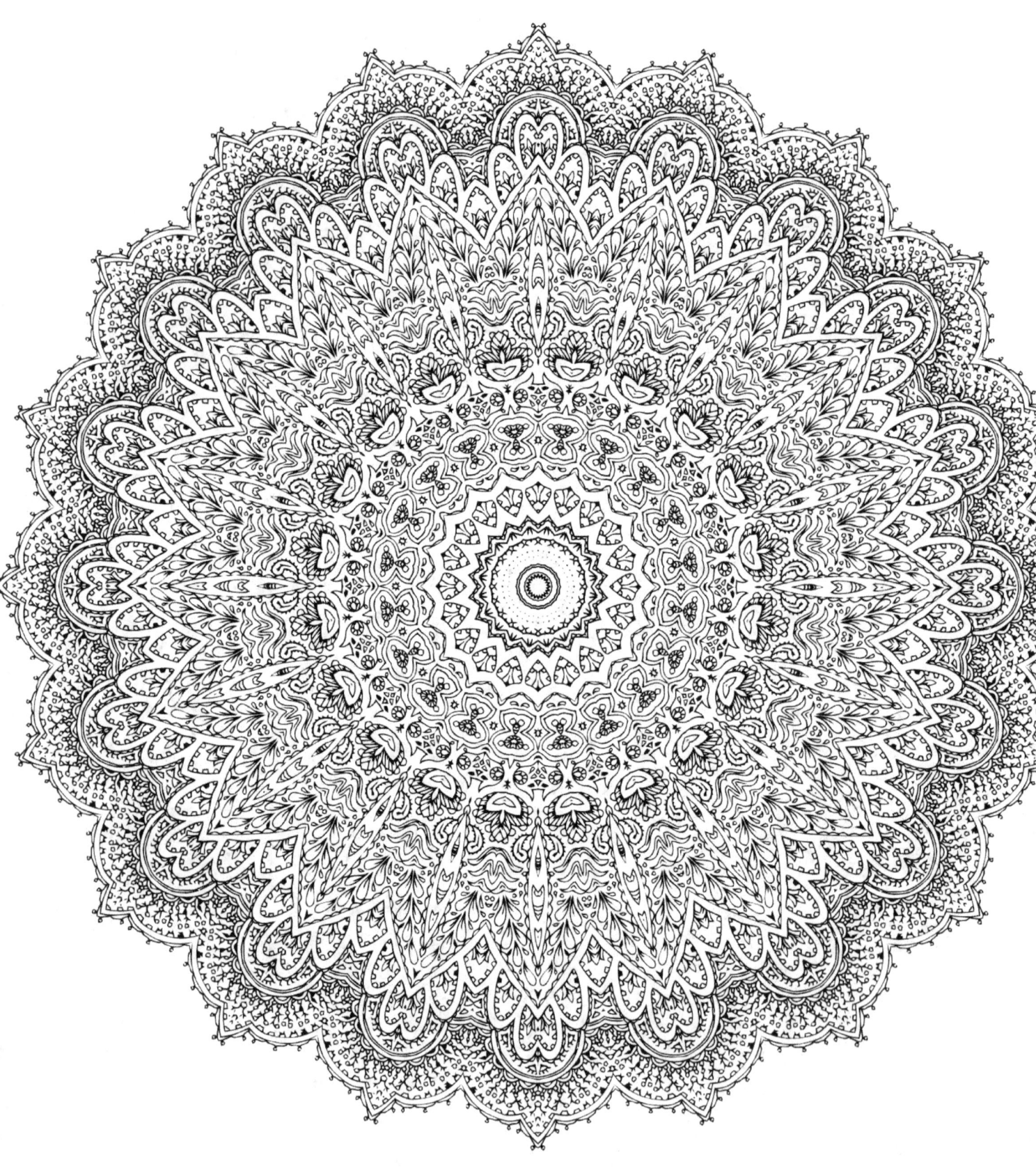

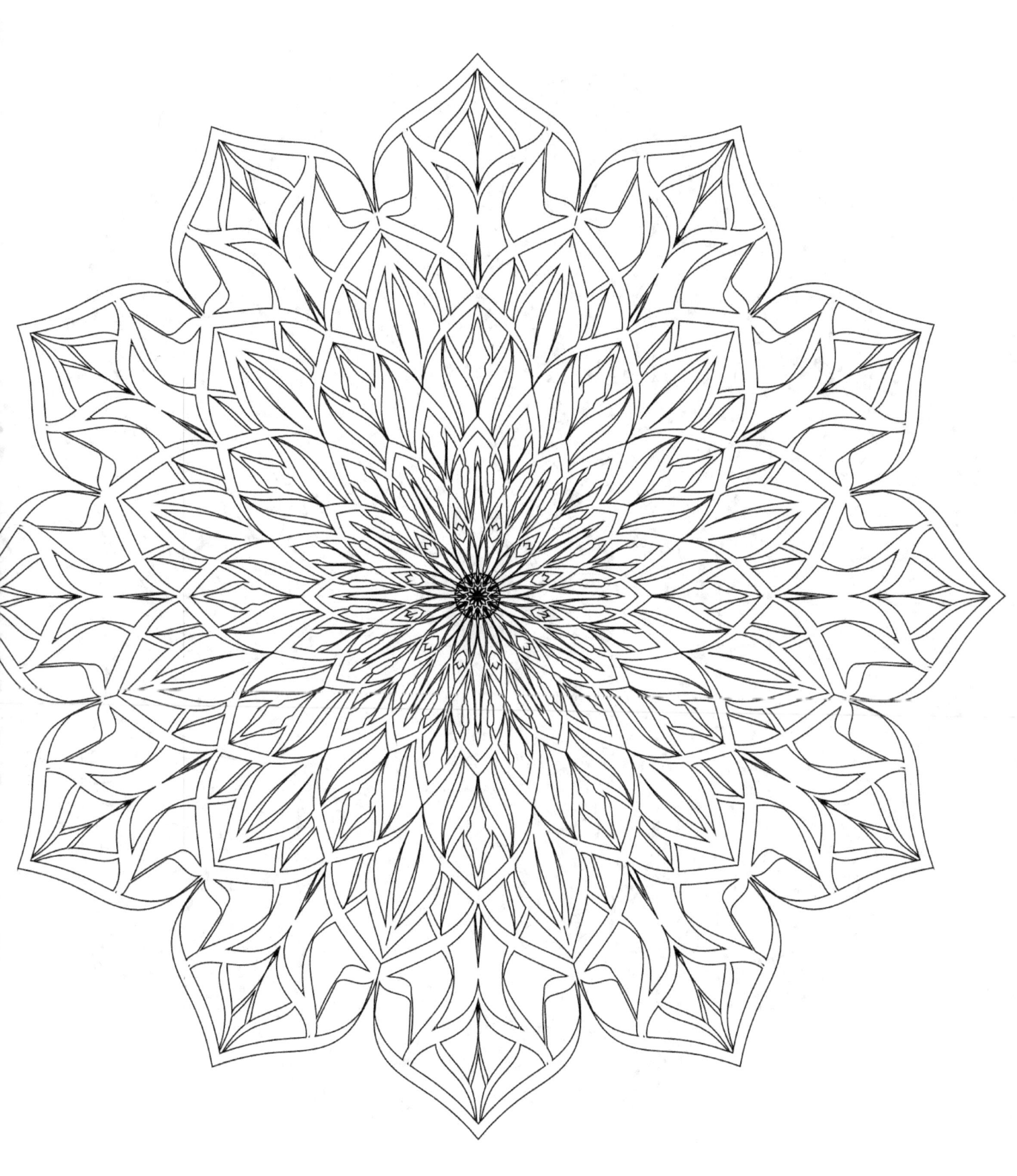

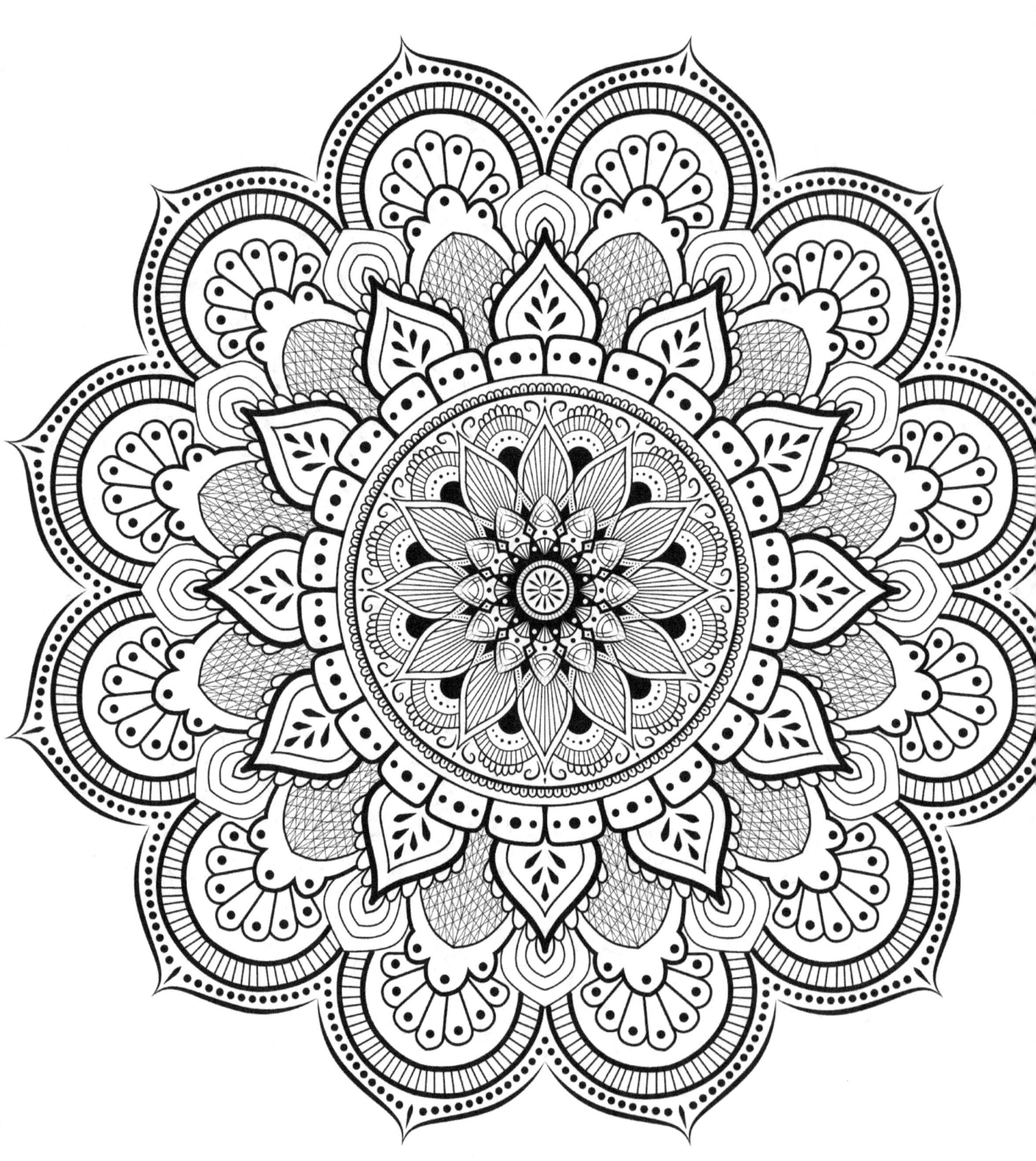

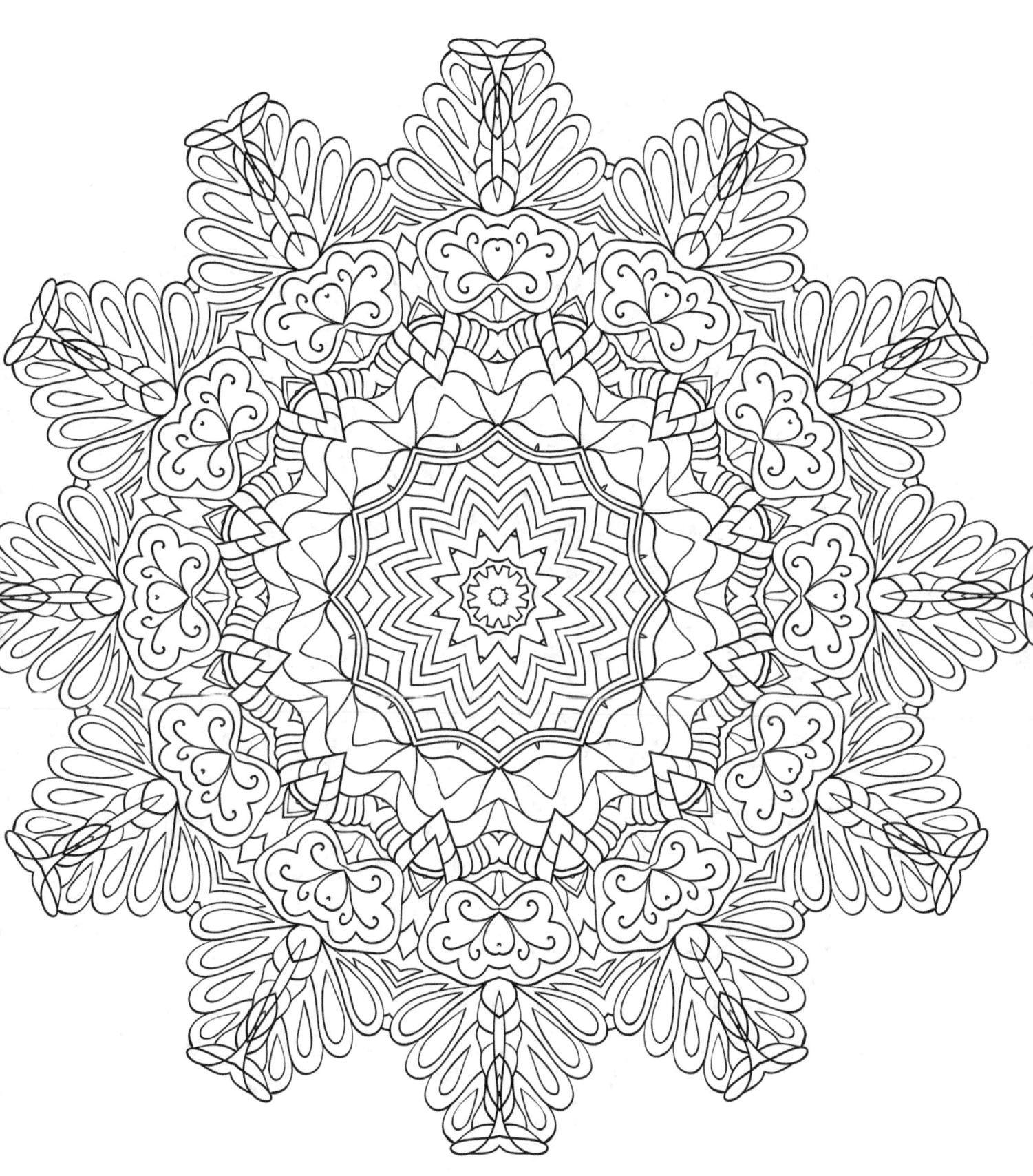

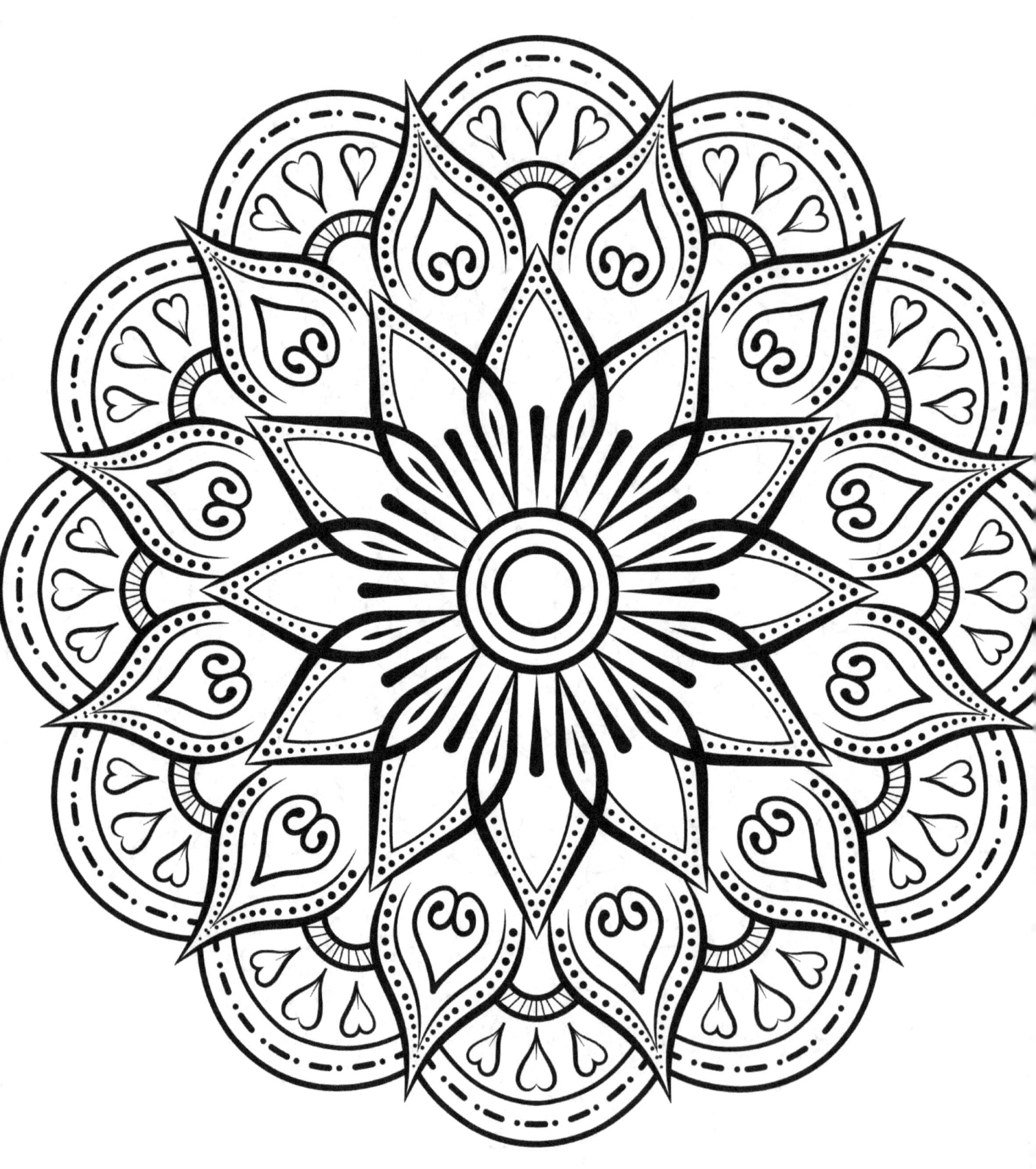

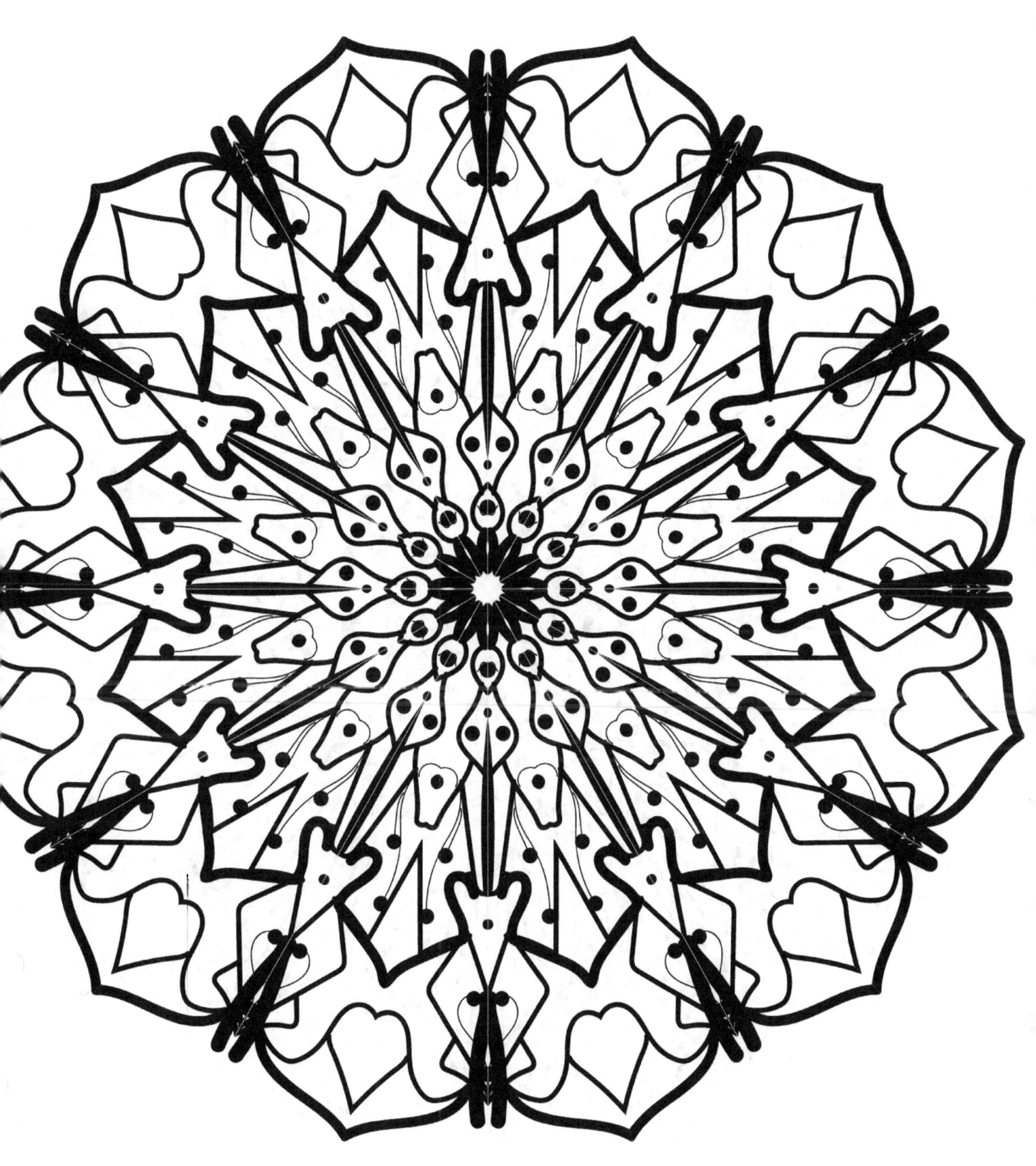

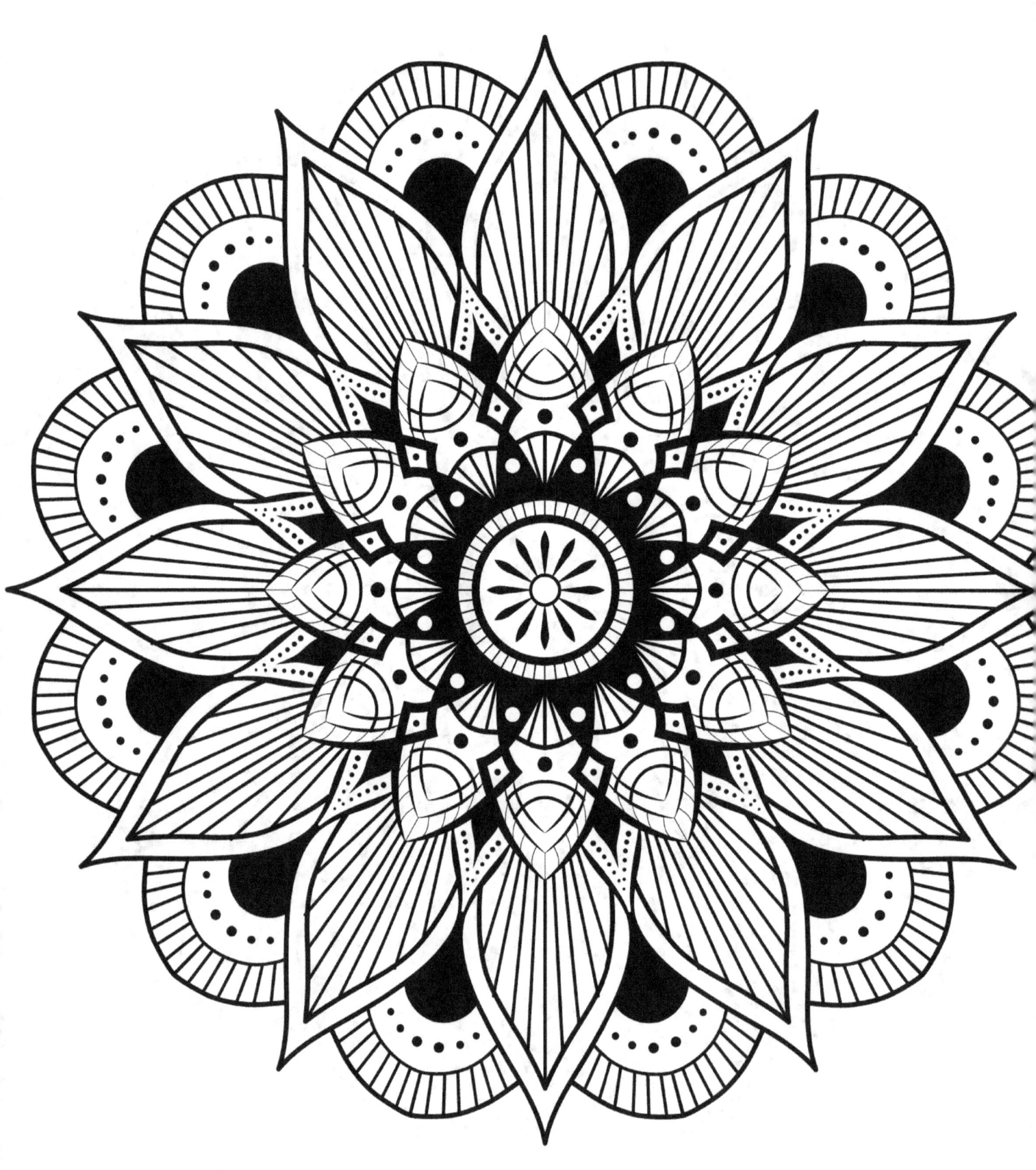

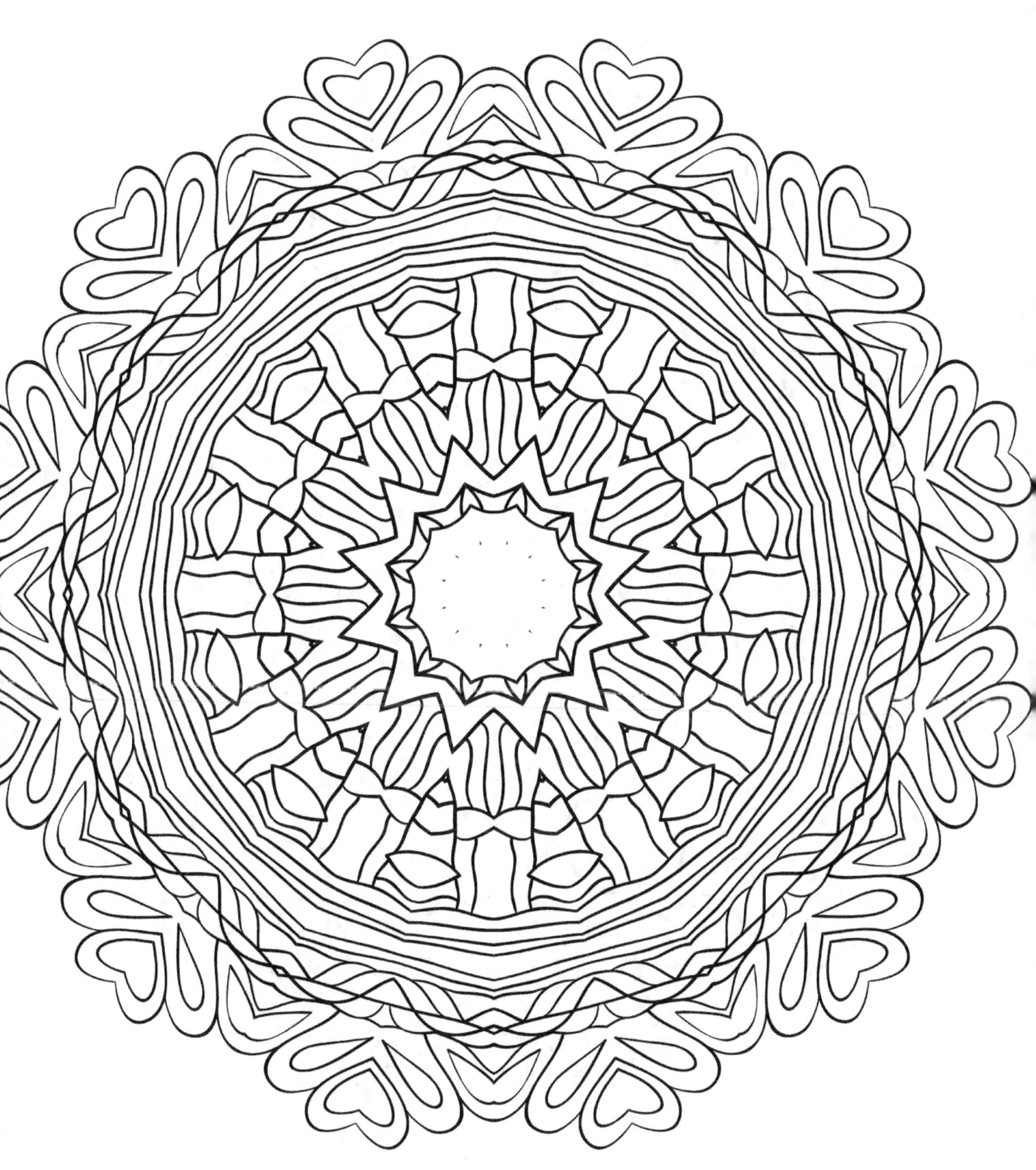

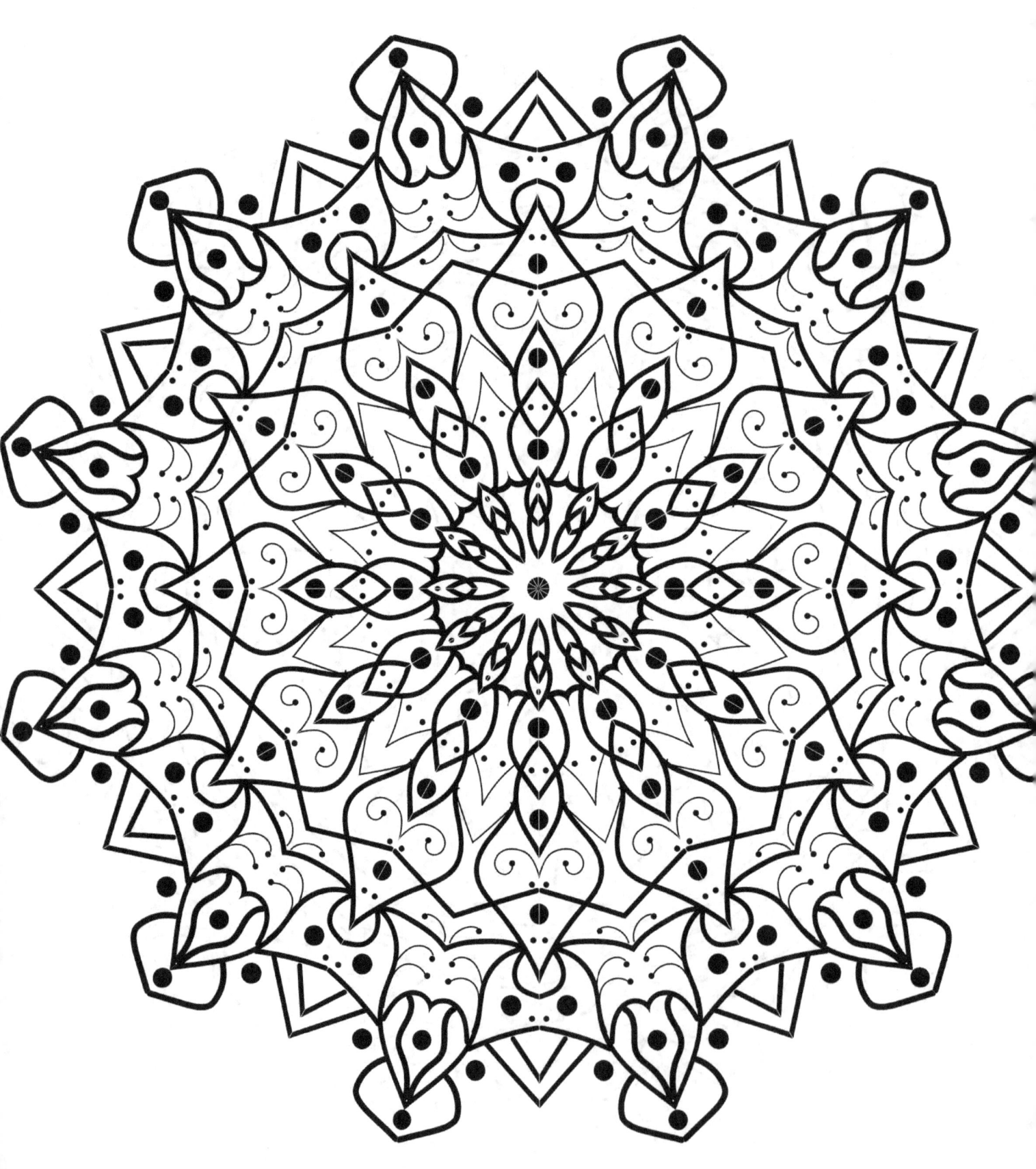

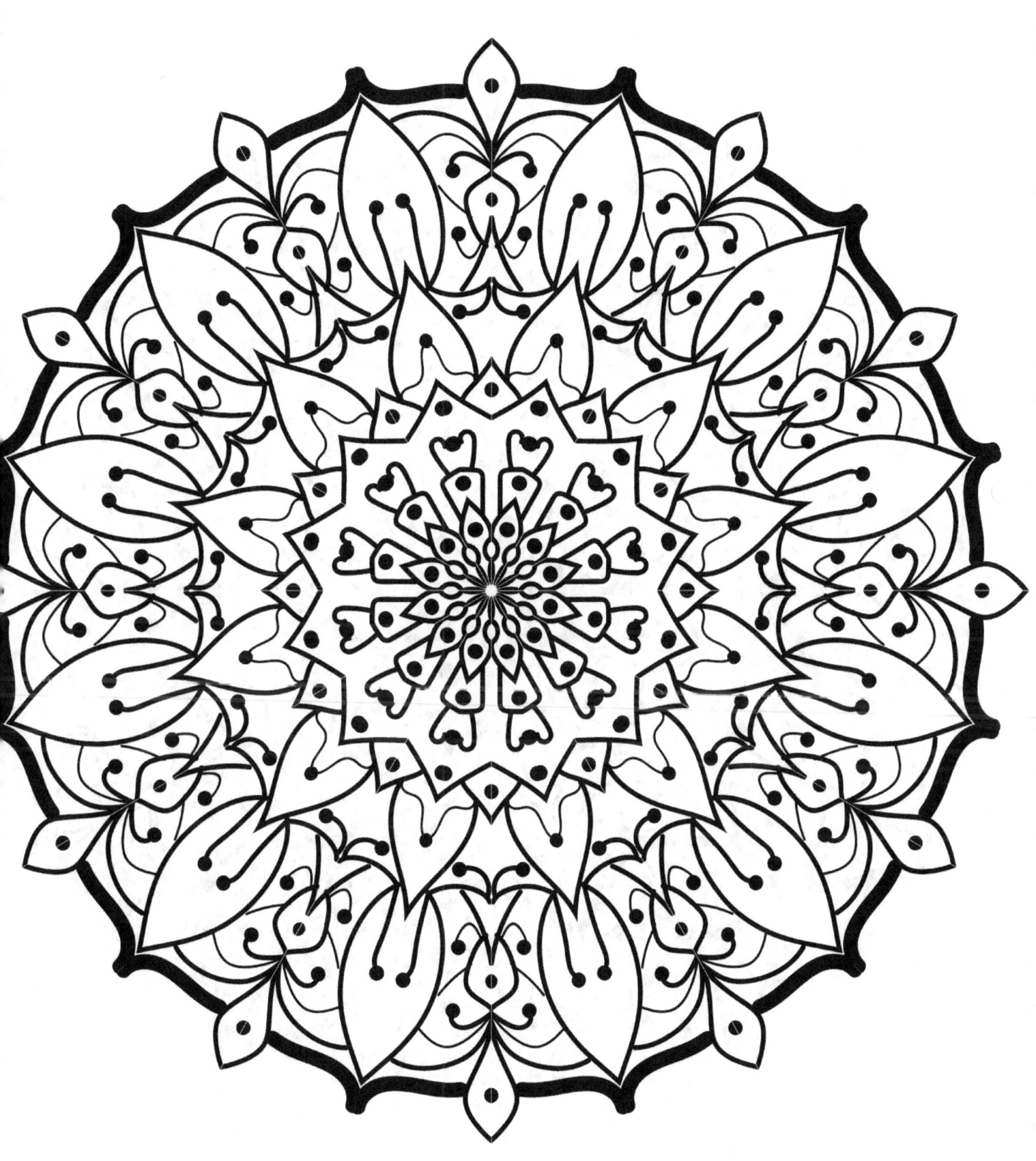

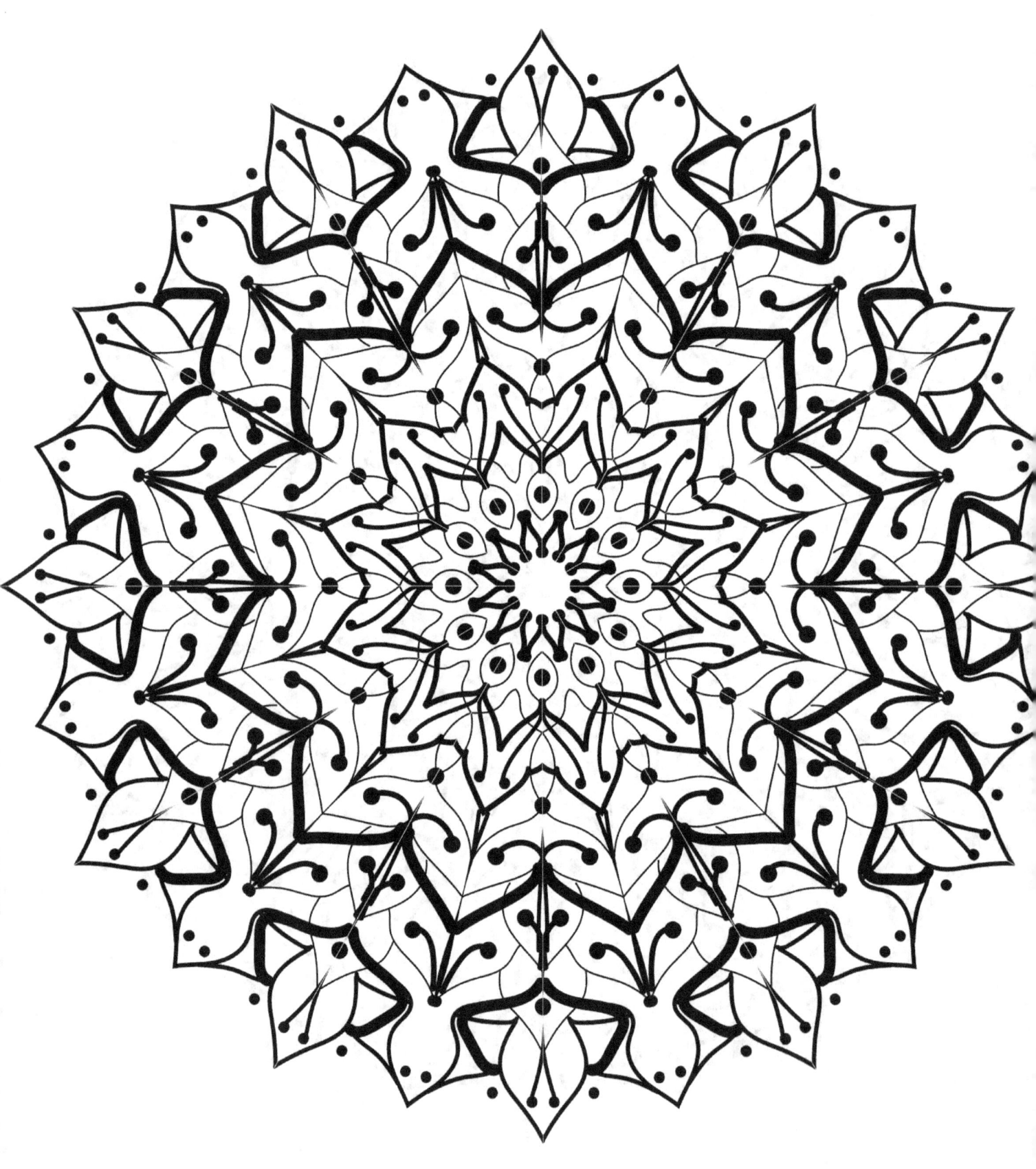